Italian Cooking for Beginners

THE ETHNIC KITCHEN

ITALIAN COOKING FOR BEGINNERS

MORE THAN 75 RECIPES FOR THE EAGER COOK

HELENE SIEGEL

ILLUSTRATIONS BY YAN NASCIMBENE

HarperCollins*Publishers*

THE ETHNIC KITCHEN: ITALIAN COOKING FOR BEGINNERS. Copyright © 1992 by Helene Siegel. All rights reserved. Printed in the United States of America. No part of this book may be used or reproduced in any manner whatsoever without written permission except in the case of brief quotations embodied in critical articles and reviews. For information, address HarperCollins Publishers, Inc., 10 East 53rd Street, New York, NY 10022.

HarperCollins books may be purchased for educational, business, or sales promotional use. For information, please call or write: Special Markets Department, HarperCollins Publishers, Inc., 10 East 53rd Street, New York, NY 10022. Telephone: (212) 207-7528; Fax: (212) 207-7222.

FIRST EDITION

Designed by Stephanie Tevonian

Library of Congress Cataloging-in-Publication Data

Siegel, Helene.
    Italian cooking for beginners : More than 75 recipes for the eager cook / Helene Siegel.
        p.   cm.   —(The Ethnic kitchen)
    Includes bibliographical references and index.
    ISBN 0-06-016429-8
    1. Cookery, Italian.   I. Title.   II. Series: Siegel, Helene. Ethnic kitchen.
TX723.S48   1992
641.5945—dc20   91-58367

92 93 94 95 96 DT/RRD 10 9 8 7 6 5 4 3 2 1

To my parents, Meyer and Ida Siegel

CONTENTS

Thanks to my agent Barbara Lowenstein and editor Susan Friedland for their belief in me and the project. And also to Patti Breitman, a constant source of support and encouragement, even if she doesn't eat meat.

Thanks to Bill Bernstein for his invaluable help in getting the computer up and running; to Jo Gruendemann for her cheerful, stalwart assistance in the kitchen; and to Ellen Rose of The Cook's Library, Los Angeles, for letting me browse too long.

The following friends shared wonderful family recipes and reminiscences: Angela and Concetta Rinaldi, Lisa Ann Marsoli, and Michael Villella.

And lastly thanks to my husband Ted and son Joey for being there to share the food and the thoughts.

How to Cook Italian Food

THE ITALIAN KITCHEN IS A WONDERFUL PLACE TO LEARN HOW TO COOK. THE INGREDIENTS ARE ACCESSIBLE, THE TECHNIQUES UNCOMPLICATED, AND THE FLAVORS FAMILIAR. IT IS HOME COOKING AT ITS BEST, WITHOUT INTRICATE GARNISHES OR FANCY SAUCES TO BURDEN THE COOK. IN FACT, IN ITALY THE COGNOSCENTI *PREFER* THE PERSONAL TOUCH OF A HOME-COOKED MEAL TO RESTAURANT COOKING.

THE OVERRIDING PRINCIPLE IS THAT THE FOOD MUST TASTE GOOD. WITH ITALIAN COOKING YOU NEED NOT STARTLE YOUR GUESTS WITH WEIRD NEW COMBINATIONS. INSTEAD YOU CAN COMBINE VEAL AND ROSEMARY, TOMATOES AND BASIL, AND PASTA AND CHEESE IN A HUNDRED DIFFERENT WAYS. EACH OF THEM WILL BE DELICIOUS.

PRESENTATION, SO IMPORTANT IN THE RESTAURANT KITCHEN, FALLS BY THE WAYSIDE WITH THIS NATURAL STYLE. IT IS MORE IMPORTANT TO SERVE THE PASTA OR RISOTTO ON A PLATE THAT RETAINS WARMTH THAN TO DRESS IT UP WITH FANCY GARNISHES OR MOLD IT INTO AN UNUSUAL SHAPE. THE BEAUTY OF INGREDIENTS SHOULD BE ALLOWED TO SHINE ON THE PLATE, WITH PERHAPS A SPRIG OF ROSEMARY OR A WEDGE OF LEMON AS ACCENT.

ITALIAN COOKING IN AMERICA HAS UNDERGONE A SEA CHANGE IN THE LAST TEN YEARS. NOW WE EMULATE THE TRADITIONAL PEASANT DIET OF GRAINS AND VEGETABLES RATHER THAN THE HEAVIER IMMIGRANT DIET. BREAD, POLENTA, RICE, PASTA, AND PIZZA ARE THE CARBOHYDRATE CARRIERS OF EXUBERANTLY FLAVORED VEGETABLES AND SMALL PORTIONS OF MEAT.

WHILE THE ITALIAN DIET IN AMERICA ONCE RELIED HEAVILY ON MEATS AND LONG-SIMMERED SAUCES, NOW THE EXCESSES HAVE BEEN PARED AWAY SO A TYPICAL ITALIAN-AMERICAN DINNER IS MORE APT TO BE ANGEL HAIR PASTA WITH FRESH TOMATOES AND BASIL THAN SPAGHETTI AND MEATBALLS.

LIKE THE BEST OF ITALIAN FURNITURE AND FASHION DESIGN, MODERN ITALIAN CUISINE IS RESTRAINED. IT DOESN'T CALL FOR TWELVE INGREDIENTS WHERE THREE WILL DO, AND LIGHTNESS IS CONSIDERED THE HIGHEST VIRTUE.

BUT ITALIAN CUISINE IS NOT ONE OF DEPRIVATION. GRILLED MEATS AND FISH AND LIGHT, UNCOOKED SAUCES ARE AS FLAVORFUL AND INVITING AS RIB-STICKING RISOTTOS AND SUBSTANTIAL SOUPS AND STEWS. ALL ARE MEANT TO BE PREPARED WITH LOVE AND EATEN WITH GUSTO IN THE ITALIAN STYLE.

A FEW TECHNIQUES
FOR THE NOVICE

Like the culture it reflects, there are very few hard and fast rules in the Italian kitchen. Here are a few principles for the time when you are ready to follow recipes less and cook more by feel.

GARLIC is used more heavily in the Italian-American kitchen than in Italy, where it is primarily associated with southern cooking.

Never brown the garlic. Cook it instead over low heat until pale yellow. When a dish calls for a combination of garlic and onion, add them to the pan at the same time and cook over low heat. This will prevent the garlic from burning and bring out the sweetness in the onion. Browned garlic is so bitter it can ruin an entire dish, so always stay nearby.

Another way to tone down raw garlic's bitterness, especially for stuffings and toppings, is to first blanch whole cloves for 2 or 3 minutes before adding to the recipe.

GARLIC, PANCETTA, AND PARSLEY are often finely chopped and then cooked over low heat at the beginning of soups or stews. This provides a flavor base of underlying complexity to even the simplest dish.

ONION, CELERY, AND CARROT are also finely chopped and cooked over low heat to provide a flavor base for braised dishes like the classic chicken cacciatore. This flavor is a little lighter than that of a dish using pancetta.

BUTTER AND OIL are often combined for sautéing over high heat. Since oil has a higher smoking point than butter, it raises the burning point in the pan. By combining the two fats you get the flavor and silkiness of butter with oil's higher smoking point. This·technique is appropriate for sautéing such fine ingredients as veal scaloppine or fish. In the Italian kitchen, butter is never clarified, as it is in the French or Indian, to raise its burning point.

TO THICKEN SAUCES that are an amalgamation of cooking juices requires long simmering or reduction. However, for sauces cooked separately, *cream or tomatoes* may be added to thicken or finish at the end of cooking time. A small amount of cream added at the end of cooking a butter-based sauce and boiled down is more in keeping with the Italian style than is a sauce using cream as its main ingredient. With olive-oil based sauces, a few tomatoes peeled, seeded, and diced and then cooked briefly at the end add body.

INSTANT "MEDITERRANEAN" FLAVORS, when used in combination, will give your cooking a light, full-bodied Mediterranean taste: olive oil, olives, tomatoes, garlic, artichokes, anchovies, capers, and such herbs as basil and rosemary.

TO PEEL AND SEED TOMATOES, trim the cores and score the bottoms with an X. Bring a pan of water to a boil and cook tomatoes for 15 seconds. Remove with a slotted spoon and immediately transfer to a bowl of cold water to stop the cooking. With a paring knife, remove the skins and cut tomatoes in half across the width. Squeeze gently to remove the seeds, or scoop them out with a teaspoon.

TO ROAST PEPPERS over a gas flame, place on burners over high heat and cook, turning occasionally, until charred all over. Transfer to a plastic bag, knot the top closed, and set aside for about 10 minutes. Rub off the charred skin and remove cores and seeds.

For the broiler method: Preheat the broiler and arrange peppers on a foil-lined baking sheet. Cook, using tongs to turn occasionally, until charred all over and then follow the same procedure for sweating and removing skins.

TO TOAST NUTS, preheat the oven to 350 F. Spread the nuts on a baking sheet and bake, shaking the pan occasionally for even cooking, 10 to 15 minutes, or until golden brown.

How to Cook Italian Food

How to Shop for Italian Cooking

GOOD ITALIAN INGREDIENTS, INCLUDING OLIVE OIL, BALSAMIC VINEGAR, AND IMPORTED PARMESAN CHEESE, ARE NOW AVAILABLE IN MOST BIG-CITY SUPERMARKETS. NONETHELESS, I RECOMMEND A TRIP TO A TRUE ITALIAN MARKET A FEW TIMES A YEAR TO STOCK UP ON REASONABLY PRICED CANS OF OLIVE OIL FOR EVERYDAY COOKING, FRESH ITALIAN SAUSAGE, HOMEMADE BREADSTICKS, AND SHEER SIMPATICO. IF YOU ARE REALLY LUCKY, MAYBE MAMA WILL STILL BE IN THE BACK MAKING SAUCES AND SOUPS FOR TAKEOUT.

A REAL ITALIAN MARKET SHOULD LOOK AS IF IT'S BEEN AROUND FOR A WHILE. THE COUNTERS SHOULD BE FORMICA, THE LIGHTING FLUORESCENT, AND THE PEOPLE BEHIND THE COUNTER SHOULD LOOK AS IF THEY ARE ON INTIMATE TERMS WITH THE MERCHANDISE. THEY SHOULD NEED NO ADVICE ON HOW TO SLICE THE PROSCIUTTO. A DISPLAY OF BRIOSCHI OR OTHER DIGESTIVE AIDS NEAR THE CASH REGISTER INDICATES YOU ARE IN THE RIGHT PLACE.

NOW FOR THE IMPORTANT PART—WHAT TO BUY. HERE IS A DESCRIPTION OF THE ITALIAN PANTRY, INCLUDING THOSE ITEMS MOST ESSENTIAL FOR DAILY COOKING. MOST ARE AVAILABLE AT THE SUPERMARKET, BUT YOU WILL FIND BETTER CHOICE AND PRICE, AS A RULE, AT AN ITALIAN MARKET.

INGREDIENTS

Note: An asterisk preceding an ingredient indicates an item recommended for daily cooking.

GRAINS

*PASTA, which should be kept on hand in as wide a variety of shapes and sizes as your cupboards will allow, is bound to be the foundation of many meals. Dry pasta, which keeps indefinitely, is always preferable to fresh except for stuffed and baked pasta dishes, like lasagne, tortellini, or ravioli. For those I recommend you find a fresh pasta shop that sells sheets and already stuffed pasta. For more information on how to cook and serve pasta, see the chapter on Pasta, Risotto, and Polenta on page 33.

SEMOLINA, the flour used for commercial pasta-making, is a coarse, pale yellow flour made from hard durum wheat. Because it cooks up firm and absorbs less water, it gives Italian pasta and pizza their characteristic chewiness. It is available in some supermarkets in the international or baking sections, or at Italian markets. Like other flours, it keeps indefinitely in a cool, dry place. I always keep a small package of semolina on hand for pizza-making.

FRESH BREAD is another must. If you do not have the time for bread-baking, locate a good source for plain white Italian bread. Local Italian bakeries deliver to some supermarkets and many delicatessens bake their own. While flavored breads made with heavier grains are currently popular, a simple crusty white loaf remains the perfect accompaniment to most Italian meals. It is essential for making grilled bruschetta, crostini, and bread crumbs, and for soaking up the delectable sauces that might otherwise remain on the plate. In Italy bread is served without butter.

*FRESH BREAD CRUMBS are made in the Italian home from leftover bread. Unlike the highly seasoned commercial Italian bread crumbs sold at the supermarket, these bland crumbs are meant to add texture and help carry other flavors rather than assert their own. To make, trim the crusts of French or Italian white bread. Dry the bread in a 300 F oven for about 30 minutes. Cut into chunks and grind in a food processor until very fine. Crumbs can be stored in sealed plastic bags or sealed containers in a cool, dry place, or in the freezer. Some Italian markets sell their own plain, unflavored bread crumbs, made from leftover bread.

ARBORIO RICE, used for making risotto, is a short, white grain that can absorb a large quantity of liquid without losing its shape. It is available at supermarkets as well as specialty stores, and can be stored indefinitely.

COARSELY GROUND CORNMEAL, used for making polenta, is available at Italian markets and some supermarkets. Do not substitute the finely ground cornmeal called for in most baking recipes. This inexpensive grain can be stored indefinitely at room temperature.

OLIVE OILS

*PURE OLIVE OIL is the most popular fat in the Italian kitchen. It is used for cooking and marinating and is the oil called for in this book unless specified. I recommend purchasing 3-liter cans of imported pure olive oil at the Italian market, where it will be much less expensive than in the supermarket. Store in a cool, dark place, not the refrigerator. For easier access, decant the oil into a plastic squeeze bottle ordinarily used for ketchup or mustard, or into a long-spouted can made for pouring oil.

EXTRA VIRGIN OLIVE OIL is a luxury ingredient. Made of the first pressing of the olives, without heat or chemicals, it is expensive and should be used with discretion. The general rule is to use virgin or extra virgin for dressings or coatings where heat will not be applied, since heat alters the flavor. I recommend keeping a small quantity on hand, especially in the summer, for salads and grilled bread.

Of all the cooking oils, olive oil has the most pronounced flavor, and extra virgin offers the purest flavor of all. A good way to taste various brands is on plain Italian bread. The best olive oils are green in color, with a distinctive olive flavor, but "best" is a very subjective thing here. Sample and decide for yourself.

Olive oil has either been processed with chemicals and heat, in which case it is "pure" or it has been cold-filtered, that is, not processed with heat, and it is "virgin" or "extra virgin." The number of extras before the word virgin is meaningless, since there are no regulations governing the use of the word in Italy or in America. With oil as with people, it is either virgin or it is not.

VINEGARS

*RED WINE VINEGAR is used in salad dressings and braised dishes to achieve the characteristic sweet and sour taste called *agrodolce*. Purchase large bottles in the supermarket and store in a cool, dry place.

*BALSAMIC VINEGAR is a special sweet Italian vinegar. It is reddish brown in color and has a heavier consistency than other vinegars. It can be purchased at supermarkets and Italian markets and can vary greatly in price, depending on whether it was aged in wooden casks according to ancient formula or sweetened more quickly with caramelized sugar. Use it sparingly in salad dressings and for drizzling on fruits and grilled vegetables. Purchase a small bottle and store in a cool, dry place.

SPICES AND CONDIMENTS

*GARLIC. Purchase large, hard knobs of garlic and store in a cool, dry place. To peel, crush individual cloves with the side of a heavy knife or cleaver and then remove the skin with your fingers. Mince garlic as finely as possible so the pieces release more flavor. Large chunks of garlic are the mark of a sloppy kitchen.

OLIVES, one of the world's oldest fruits, are an integral part of the southern Italian diet. In all of the cooking of the Mediterranean, olives are not only eaten out of hand as a snack food but are also cooked with meat, fish, poultry, and vegetables. They even appear as a main ingredient in spreads like olivada and sauces like bagna cauda.

American pitted, processed olives, however, are a pale substitute for olives prepared according to the old, slow methods of washing and pickling. In their rush to remove the pits, our food processors have also removed the flavor.

California black olives, sold in the can, are actually unripened or green olives that have been chemically blackened and then treated with lye and pitted mechanically—a method developed because the flesh of ripe, black olives is too soft to withstand machine-pitting. Pitted green olives also lack the nuance of flavor and intensity of a green Sicilian or a tiny Pitchouline from France.

There is a wide variety of wonderful black and green olives sold in bulk at Italian and other ethnic markets as well as specialty shops like cheese and gourmet shops. In addition, some American companies like Santa Barbara Olive Company and Peloponnese, are distributing delicious real olives to some supermarkets.

The best way to learn about olives is to buy a selection and taste. For these recipes, as a rule, black Kalamata olives, imported from Greece, are recommended. When cooking with green olives, be wary of the Sicilian type, as they are extremely garlicky and may overpower other flavors. Try a country-style or perhaps a French green olive for cooking and blanch it first if the flavor is too overpowering to use in combination. All olives should be stored in the refrigerator in their brine, where they will keep indefinitely.

*CAPERS are the unopened buds of a small bush that grows wild along the Mediterranean. After being picked, they are pickled in salted white vinegar, where they develop their characteristic salty, acidic taste. They play an important role in Sicilian cooking and are often combined with raisins or currants for a sweet and sour effect. The best are the imported small nonpareil type, available in bottles at the supermarket. Larger capers, though less expensive, are tougher to chew and extremely pungent. Opened jars of capers should be stored in their brine in the refrigerator.

*ANCHOVIES are small fish cured in oil and used primarily as an accent or garnish. Along the Mediterranean they are also sold and eaten as a fresh fish, as are sardines. Imported anchovies, available at Italian markets, are packed in salt and olive oil and sold in reclosable glass jars, much more convenient to store than tins. They keep, packed in oil, in the refrigerator indefinitely.

*MARINATED ARTICHOKE HEARTS lend a Mediterranean flavor to pizzas and pasta dishes. They are available at the supermarket or in bulk at the Italian market and can be stored in the refrigerator, in their oil, indefinitely.

*RED PEPPER FLAKES are the dried seeds and membranes of the red chile pepper; they appear on the counter in pizza shops. They are available in the spice section at the supermarket. Heat releases their intense power so use with discretion.

PORK PRODUCTS

PROSCIUTTO is ham cured in a traditional long, slow process with salt and air only. It is unsmoked and contains no nitrates or preservatives. Its distinctive sweet, salty taste is prized in Italy and America, where it is quite expensive. Always purchase either the amount you need for a recipe or what you plan on eating within the next day or two, as properly sliced prosciutto dries out quickly.

It is available, both domestic and imported, at some supermarkets in the deli case, as well as in specialty stores. Although the most prized variety, cured in Parma, is now available in the United States, it is an extravagance. For most recipes a moderately priced imported variety is fine. Unless the recipe states otherwise, it is best sliced paper-thin and packed between sheets of wax paper. If you do not plan on using it right away, wrap the paper-wrapped ham in aluminium foil for storage in the refrigerator.

In Italy, prosciutto is most often eaten plain on an antipasto platter, or even for breakfast with some slivers of good Parmesan, bread, and fruit. It should never be cooked until crisp.

PANCETTA, from the belly of the pig, is the same cut as bacon. The unsmoked meat is combined with fat, salt, and spices and then rolled to form a log. Used widely as a flavor base for soups, stews, and fricassees, pancetta is less expensive than prosciutto.

Pancetta is available at Italian markets and specialty shops. It is less perishable than prosciutto and can be stored, well wrapped, in the refrigerator for a couple of weeks, or even frozen. Because of its high fat content it can be difficult to slice and chop, especially at room temperature. If your recipe calls for pancetta to be chopped or minced, try purchasing it in ¼-inch-thick slices. They will be easier to work with. Pancetta is often combined with garlic and parsley at the beginning of long-simmered soups and braised dishes.

CHEESES

*****PARMESAN** cheese is a constant in Italian cooking. It adds body and flavor to pasta, pizza, egg and vegetable dishes, risottos, and soups. Imported Parmesan, of which the best is Parmigiano-Reggiano, is pale gold in color and has a crumbly dry texture. In Italy, special short knives have been developed for breaking off pieces downward, along the natural grain.

Since it is so expensive, I do not recommend Reggiano for everyday cooking, although it is nice to buy a piece for tasting. Other imported Parmesans are fine, and although I know it is blasphemy, hand-grating is not necessary either. If you do not have the time, just buy a good cheese in moderate quantity at a local cheese shop or Italian market and have it grated there. At home, store in the refrigerator in a sealed plastic container. If you buy enough for about 3 weeks it won't dry out. In any case, it will certainly beat the grated Parmesan sold at the supermarket. Well-wrapped chunks of Parmesan may be stored in the freezer for a long time.

The food processor can be used for grating Parmesan and other hard cheeses at home. First bring the cheese to room temperature and then cut into 1-inch cubes. Process with the metal blade until fine.

MOZZARELLA. This mild, white melting cheese is indispensable for making pizza. The fresh variety, still made from buffalo's milk in Italy, is available in cheese shops and some Italian markets. Because it is quite expensive and perishable, I do not recommend imported fresh mozzarella. Purchase instead fresh domestic mozzarella, made from cow's milk. It is available in small balls *(bocconcini)*, packed in water, at some supermarkets and specialty shops. It also is quite perishable, so check the expiration date for freshness. Always store in the refrigerator, packed in water.

When you need a large quantity, say for melting on pizzas, buy 1-pound mozzarella balls. Try a few brands until you find the softest and tastiest and always grate before melting. Although it is available at the supermarket, you may find better brands at an Italian market.

RICOTTA is like a soft, sweet cottage cheese. It is used in several stuffed pasta dishes, in desserts, and as a breakfast cheese.

ROMANO, or Pecorino Romano, is another hard grating and melting cheese similar to Parmesan. It is paler in color than Parmesan and has a saltier, more assertive flavor. Use as you would Parmesan.

GORGONZOLA, a soft blue-veined cheese, is usually eaten out of hand. It also is used in pasta dishes, antipasti, and desserts, usually in combination with fruit, pear being the classic accompaniment at the end of the meal. Gorgonzola is available at cheese and Italian markets where they may stock two varieties, picante and dolce latte, a sweeter, creamier variety.

FONTINA, a pale yellow, semisoft cheese from Italy's Alpine region, is often matched with veal. It melts beautifully and has a nuttier, fuller flavor than mozzarella without being as assertive as Parmesan. American and Danish fontina have quite different flavors from Italian, so do not substitute. For the Italian variety, try an Italian market or well-stocked cheese shop.

MASCARPONE is a soft, sweet, white cream cheese used mainly in desserts, like the popular tiramisù. Whether imported or domestic, it has a short shelf life, so always check the expiration date and use quickly. It is available in some supermarkets in the gourmet cheese section, and in cheese shops.

VEGETABLES

Italian farmers are legendary for their ability to coax a wide variety of beautiful vegetables from even the rockiest soil. And Italian cooks honor them by cooking vegetables cleanly and simply, so their true flavors are revealed.

The vegetables most closely associated with the Italian kitchen are red and green bell peppers, eggplant, fennel, zucchini, tomato, and certain lettuces. Some of my personal favorites among the greens are arugula, watercress, escarole or chicory, and Belgian endive. The best dressing for such an Italian salad is a mixture of half lemon juice and half extra virgin olive oil with a dash of salt and pepper.

TOMATOES, technically a fruit, define Italian cuisine for much of the world. This native of South America was brought to Italy in the late sixteenth century and did not start being used widely until the end of the next century, especially in the south, where it still enjoys its greatest popularity.

Here in the United States, the supermarket tomato has taken such a downturn that except for the summer months, cooks are better off with the canned product. When they are in the market, small, Italian plum tomatoes, or Roma, hold less water and are tastier than the larger round tomatoes. However, because of their size, they are not recommended for cooking in quantity.

For sauce-making and quick cooking, especially when tomatoes are out of season, keep on hand three types of canned tomatoes as well as tomato paste. *Peeled tomatoes*, packed in their juices along with a leaf of basil, are good for dishes where you want to control the texture. Since they are only peeled, they are the least cooked of the canned varieties.

Crushed tomatoes have been peeled, partially seeded, and chopped. They save time and because of their chunky texture add body. *Tomato purée* is a thick liquid that is slightly precooked. It is the least desirable for cooking.

Tomato paste should be used sparingly, as its intense flavor is difficult to balance with other, fresher flavors. Try to purchase the imported type, packed in a tube like toothpaste, and available at specialty stores. It is easier to use a small amount at a time and save the rest.

HERBS

The general rule for substituting dry herbs for fresh is to use one-third to one-half the quantity. Since heat releases the flavor and fresh herbs are fragile, add fresh herbs near the end of cooking time. Dry herbs should be added at the beginning so they have more time to release their flavor.

I am partial to fresh herbs but I live in California where they are easily grown and even more easily bought at the supermarket.

ITALIAN PARSLEY, the flat-leafed variety sold in supermarkets, has a more delicate bitter flavor and finer texture than the curly type. The most popular herb in the Italian kitchen, it is used in every part of the meal except dessert, and often is combined with pancetta and garlic as a flavor base. It is an easy herb to grow or to find in the store.

*BASIL has a dark green, soft leaf and subtle, sweet licorice-like flavor. It is the classic herb for flavoring tomatoes and the main ingredient in pesto sauce. Since it only keeps a few days in the refrigerator, do not purchase far in advance. This popular herb is available nearly year-round at the supermarket. Some gardeners find it easy to grow, although I have had little luck in the intense heat of California summers.

ROSEMARY leaves resemble short, thick pine needles. Because of their thick, chewy texture they need to be minced quite fine or added as a whole sprig that can be removed before serving. Rosemary goes well with poultry, veal, lamb, and pork, and is used as a flavoring for breads. It is a very hearty, drought-resistant plant that grows wild in parts of California. The dry herb can always be substituted.

SAGE has a pale green, fuzzy leaf and a strong, distinctive flavor with an aroma reminiscent of camphor. It usually is matched with poultry, pork, and veal and is the classic flavoring in the dish saltimbocca.

*OREGANO AND MARJORAM may be used interchangeably in Italian cooking, since the tastes are so similar. Oregano is one of the few herbs used more often dry than fresh, and it is frequently used in tomato sauces and stews. Keep a large bottle of the dried herb in the pantry.

The other herbs called for in Italian cooking are **BAY LEAVES** and fresh **SPEARMINT** for Mediterranean-style cooking.

FRUITS

*LEMONS, both juice and zest (the yellow part of the skin), play an important role in heightening the fresh flavors of Italian cooking. Sicily, where the fruit is even eaten out of hand as a snack, is the world's largest producer of lemons.

Look for thin-skinned lemons that yield to pressure when squeezed with a thumb. Store at room temperature and as a general rule add lemon juice toward the end of cooking so the flavor does not get cooked away. Electric citrus juicers and old-fashioned hand reamers work well, but for really fast cooking here is the method chefs use. Press down with your palm and roll the lemon on the counter first. Then slice in half across the width and spear with a fork in the center, squeezing and twisting to release the juice.

Do not use the lemon juice sold in bottles or plastic lemons at the supermarket. Real lemon juice is too ephemeral to last on the shelf, so other ingredients like coconut oil and cocoa butter have to be added to approximate the real thing. It doesn't come close.

EQUIPMENT FOR THE ITALIAN KITCHEN

You may not need to buy anything to start cooking Italian. All it really takes is a few good knives, some pots and pans, and a colander. Here are the essentials and a few less than essential but marvelous tools to make your time in the kitchen go more smoothly.

For pasta-making you should have an *8- to 10-quart straight-edge pot* with sturdy handles and a lid. Avoid buying enameled cast-iron cookware for this purpose as the pot will be too heavy once it is filled with water and pasta. The best *colanders* for draining pasta have feet on the bottom so they can stand in the sink while you use both hands to pour in the pasta. Buy the largest size that fits in your sink for cooking large quantities of pasta.

Another essential for cooking pasta is a comfortable bowl in which to serve it. Look for a *low, wide ceramic bowl* specifically made for that purpose. It makes pasta-tossing easier and prevents sauce from settling to the bottom.

For sautéing, roasting, and braising *a medium and a large sauté pan, a roasting pan with lid, and a heavy dutch oven* should do just fine.

Long-handled tongs for moving hot foods, wooden spoons for stirring, and a squeeze bottle or oil can for drizzling olive oil are the only other essentials.

For home pizza-making there are two special pieces of equipment: *a wooden peel or paddle and a pizza stone.* The peel, designed for reaching into a very hot oven, reduces the risk of your beautiful pizza falling apart on its way into the oven.

The pizza stone simulates a wood-burning oven by quickly drawing out moisture and crisping the crust. Of the many brands available I recommend nonasbestos concrete, the same material the revolving decks in professional pizza ovens are made of. They do not need to be soaked in water like quarry tiles or specially treated to withstand a 500 F oven. They are available, cut in slabs to fit the home oven, by mail from: Ed La Dou, Caioti Restaurant, 2100 Laurel Canyon Boulevard, Los Angeles, California 90046.

The last piece of equipment is a good coffee maker. Electric drip coffee makers, manuals like Melitta or the imported Moka or

Napoletano in conjunction with good, dark beans are all fine for making Italian-style coffee. An Italian chef I know combines half espresso and half Colombian beans for his family's kitchen. For *caffè latte,* just mix half strong coffee with heated milk.

If you have room in your kitchen, an espresso/cappuccino maker might be nice. However, if you view cappuccino as I do, as an excuse for people-watching, you will resist the temptation to bring another appliance into your life.

Italian Cooking for Beginners

SOUPS AND
ANTIPASTI

Here are a few peasant soups and simple appetizers for beginning the meal. When Italians entertain at home the antipasto course is often a casual selection of items from the delicatessen as well as homemade specialties. A platter of cold cuts like prosciutto, mortadella, and salami; figs or cantaloupe slices delicately wrapped with prosciutto; some roasted peppers; a selection of olives and slivers of Parmesan garnished with lemon wedges, breadsticks, and good country bread set the tone for the naturally good tastes to follow.

TUSCAN WHITE BEAN SOUP

This hearty bean soup captures the tradition of rustic simplicity Tuscans are known for—and their love of beans. It makes a delightful winter supper with a glass of red wine and Crostini (see page 25).

Serves 8

1 pound dry white beans, such as Great Northern or cannellini
¼ cup olive oil
¼ pound pancetta, finely chopped
3 garlic cloves, peeled and minced
1 onion, peeled and diced
2 celery ribs, thinly sliced
2 tablespoons chopped fresh Italian parsley
1 teaspoon salt
½ teaspoon white pepper
5½ cups chicken stock or canned broth
Reserved cooking liquid from beans
2 sprigs fresh rosemary
2 tomatoes, peeled, seeded, and diced
2 tablespoons extra virgin olive oil

1] Place the beans in a colander and rinse in cold water to remove any grit. Then place in a large saucepan and add enough water to cover generously. Bring to a boil, reduce to a simmer, and cook, uncovered, until the beans just lose their starchy flavor, about 1 hour. Strain the beans, reserving the cooking water. The beans and the water may be reserved, in covered bowls, up to 6 hours at room temperature.

2] In a stockpot, heat the olive oil over medium-low heat. Add the pancetta and garlic and cook until the garlic is lightly colored, about 3 minutes. Add the onion, celery, parsley, salt, and pepper. Cook over low heat until the vegetables are soft, about 10 minutes.

3] Pour in the chicken broth, the reserved liquid from the beans, rosemary sprigs, and beans. Bring to a boil, reduce to a simmer, and cook, uncovered, 1 hour. Occasionally skim and discard the foam that rises to the top. The beans should be soft and buttery, without any starchiness, when done.

4] Remove the rosemary sprigs and discard. Stir in the diced tomatoes and extra virgin olive oil and simmer an additional 5 minutes just to heat through. Serve hot.

WINTER MINESTRONE SOUP

———————————— ■ ————————————

Dice the vegetables as fine as you can for the proper consistency, and serve with a generous dollop of pesto or grated Parmesan cheese and toasted Italian bread. Grilled chops or a very simple roast are all you need for a meal beginning with such a flavorful soup. ✗ *Serves 6 to 8*

½ cup dry white beans, Great Northern or cannellini
1 large onion, peeled and diced
2 carrots, peeled and diced
2 celery ribs, diced
2 medium red potatoes, with skins, diced
2 large zucchini, diced
½ pound green beans, trimmed and cut into ½-inch lengths
3 tomatoes, peeled, seeded, and diced
¼ pound pancetta

4 garlic cloves, peeled
12 sprigs fresh Italian parsley, stems removed
2 tablespoons olive oil
5 cups canned chicken broth
5 cups liquid (see Step 5)
½ cup tubetti, semi de melone, or other small pasta
¼ cup chopped fresh basil
Salt and freshly ground pepper
Grated Parmesan cheese or Pesto (see page 52) for garnish

1] Place beans in a colander and rinse with cold water to remove any dirt. Transfer to a medium saucepan, cover generously with water, and bring to a boil. Reduce to a simmer and cook, uncovered, about 1 hour, or until beans lose their starchy taste. (The beans are very absorbent so keep checking the pot and adding water as needed. They should always be covered with water.)

2] While the beans are softening, clean and chop all the vegetables. Since this is the labor-intensive part of making vegetable soup, I like to do all the chopping at once and then arrange the ingredients in bowls near the stove.

3] Roughly chop the pancetta. In a food processor fitted with the metal blade, combine pancetta, peeled garlic, and parsley. Process into a rough paste by pulsing on/off about 20 times.

4] In a large stockpot, heat the olive oil over moderate heat. Add the pancetta and garlic paste and cook about 4 minutes, stirring frequently with a wooden spoon to avoid scorching.

5] Pour in the chicken broth. Strain the beans and reserve the cooking water. Add to the stockpot 5 cups of liquid consisting of water from the beans plus cold water as needed. Also add the softened beans. Bring to a boil, reduce to a simmer, and cook, uncovered, 15 minutes. With a ladle, remove the foam or impurities that rise to the top.

6] Add the onion, carrots, celery, and potatoes. Bring back to a boil, reduce to a simmer and cook, uncovered, about 20 minutes. Then add the zucchini and green beans. Boil and simmer, uncovered, an additional 15 minutes. Keep skimming foam between additions.

7] Bring a small saucepan of salted water to a boil. Cook the tubetti or other pasta just short of al dente. Drain and reserve.

8] To the stockpot add the cooked pasta, tomatoes, and basil. Simmer an additional 5 minutes and season conservatively with salt and pepper, since Parmesan or pesto will be added at the table.

ABOUT VEGETABLE SOUPS

☞ THE KEY TO A DELICIOUS VEGETABLE SOUP IS TO BEGIN WITH BEAUTIFUL, FRESH VEGETABLES, NOT WITHERED ONES FROM THE BACK OF THE REFRIGERATOR. COOKING OLD VEGETABLES WILL NOT IMPROVE THEIR TASTE.

ALWAYS ADD HARD VEGETABLES FIRST SO THEY COOK LONGER AND THE SOFTER ONES AT THE END FOR A BRIEFER COOKING TIME. LIKE ALL VEGETABLE SOUPS, ITALIAN MINESTRONE INVITES IMPROVISATION. WHILE THIS VERSION, WITH ITS BEANS, POTATOES, AND PASTA, IS APPROPRIATE FOR WINTER, YOU CAN OMIT ANY OF THE STARCHES AND LIGHTEN IT FOR SPRING OR SUMMER WITH SEASONAL VEGETABLES LIKE ASPARAGUS AND CORN. THIS PARTICULAR VERSION IMPROVES WITH A FEW DAYS IN THE REFRIGERATOR.

ESCAROLE ORZO SOUP

Since there are so few ingredients, the quality of the broth *will* make a difference in this light, refreshing soup. It is best made with rich homemade chicken broth, but if you must substitute, mix half canned broth with half water and then season to taste.

Escarole, a faintly bitter salad green also known as chicory, is a staple of the Italian-American kitchen. It is available at the supermarket in the lettuce section. ✗ *Serves 6 to 8*

8 cups rich homemade chicken broth
½ cup orzo or other small pasta

1 medium head (1 pound) escarole, washed
Freshly grated Parmesan cheese

1] Bring the chicken broth to a boil in a large stockpot. Add the orzo, reduce to a low boil, and cook 5 minutes. Skim off and discard the starch or foam that rises to the top.

2] Meanwhile stack the clean escarole leaves and roughly chop into small pieces. Add to the broth and cook, uncovered, at a gentle simmer about 7 minutes. Serve hot with plenty of grated Parmesan cheese.

COOKING WITH BEANS

☞ IN ANY RECIPE CALLING FOR DRIED BEANS, INSTEAD OF SOAKING, YOU CAN BOIL THEM FOR 1 HOUR IN A GENEROUS POT OF UNSALTED WATER TO SOFTEN. TO TEST FOR DONENESS, CHOOSE THE DENSEST BEAN AND BITE INTO IT. AS SOON AS THE STARCHY TASTE IS GONE, THE BEANS ARE DONE. CANNED BEANS CAN ALWAYS BE SUBSTITUTED FOR DRY: RINSE THEM TO REMOVE EXCESS SALT AND ADD TO RECIPES AT THE END, JUST TO HEAT THROUGH.

BRUSCHETTA AND CROSTINI

Bruschetta is Italian garlic bread before it got modernized with bizarre ingredients like imitation butter and processed garlic. It is simply good crusty country bread, thickly sliced and grilled and then brushed with olive oil and rubbed with garlic.

When the grilled bread is topped with a savory spread, it is called crostini, and is served as a starter or antipasto. In addition to the toppings that follow, crostini is delicious smeared with Pesto (see page 52), the Baked Garlic Tomatoes on page 99, or the black olive paste in the recipe on page 49.

For summer parties, try arranging slices of grilled bread in a basket along with a few crocks of roasted garlic cloves and spreads for guests to choose from.

1 large loaf Italian country bread, avoid those with strong flavorings like olives or nuts

Extra virgin olive oil
Garlic cloves, peeled and crushed

1] Preheat the grill or oven to 450 F. Slice the bread into ½-inch slices and grill until golden and toasty. Although a blackened spot here or there is nice, do not totally blacken the bread. If you are using the oven, spread the slices on a baking sheet and bake about 4 minutes per side.

2] Brush the warm bread with olive oil and rub gently with a crushed garlic clove. (The first time I did this I rubbed so madly the bread got bitter from the garlic, so be careful.)

3] For crostini, skip the garlic unless you can't help yourself, and serve with assorted toppings.

WHITE BEANS WITH GARLIC

✗ *Makes 1 cup, enough for 4 large crostini*

3 tablespoons extra virgin olive oil
1 garlic clove, peeled and minced
One 15-ounce can cannellini
  (white kidney beans)

Salt and white pepper
Fresh lemon juice

1] In a small skillet over low heat, heat the oil. Cook the garlic about 5 minutes.

2] Drain and rinse the beans. Add to the pan along with salt and pepper. Cook, stirring frequently, until the beans break down and are heated through, 7 minutes. Mash to a rough consistency with the tines of a fork.

3] Season to taste with lemon juice and remove from heat. Serve warm spread on crostini, or reserve in the refrigerator and bring back to room temperature before serving.

MARINATED TOMATOES

✗ *Makes 1¾ cups*

4 Italian plum tomatoes, diced
1 garlic clove, peeled and minced
½ cup extra virgin olive oil

2 tablespoons chopped fresh basil
1 teaspoon coarse salt
Freshly ground black pepper

Combine the ingredients in a small bowl. Cover and let marinate at room temperature at least 1 hour. Spoon on crostini.

RICOTTA AND CHIVES

✗ *Makes 2 cups*

One 15-ounce container ricotta
  cheese
2 tablespoons extra virgin olive oil
¾ cup chopped Kalamata olives

3 tablespoons minced chives
1 tablespoon minced scallions
Salt and white pepper

Mix in a bowl with a fork and chill up to 1 hour. Serve as a spread.

PANZANELLA

In the original version of this peasant dish, old bread was softened with water and then placed beneath the salad where it soaked up the dressing and became a little swamp—or panzanella. Here good Italian bread, preferably a white country loaf, is toasted with olive oil and garlic and then added to the salad like croutons. If you don't plan on using the grill for another purpose, the bread can be done in a hot oven or on a high setting in the toaster. You can mix the vegetables and dressing a few hours in advance but add the bread cubes right before serving for the best texture. ✕ *Serves 6*

4 large tomatoes
½ large red onion, peeled and diced
1½ tablespoons chopped fresh basil
2 or 3 pickling cucumbers, peeled and trimmed
¼ cup red wine vinegar

½ cup extra virgin olive oil
1 garlic clove, peeled and minced
½ teaspoon coarse salt
Freshly ground black pepper
Two ½-inch slices Bruschetta (see page 25), or toasted Italian bread

1] Trim the stems and cut the unpeeled tomatoes in half across the width. With a teaspoon scoop out and discard the seeds and roughly chop the flesh. Place in a shallow salad or pasta bowl along with the red onion and basil.

2] Cut the cucumbers in quarters lengthwise and then in ¼-inch slices across the width. Add to the tomato mixture.

3] In a small mixing bowl, whisk together the vinegar, olive oil, garlic, salt, and pepper. Pour over the salad and toss to combine.

4] Immediately before serving, cut the toasted bruschetta into ½-inch cubes. Add to the salad, toss to combine, and adjust the seasonings to taste. Serve at room temperature within the hour.

MARINATED ROASTED RED PEPPERS

Roasted red peppers are an important part of an antipasto selection. Their bright red color and delicate sweetness refresh the eye and provide a welcome contrast to stronger, more savory foods. Peppers can be prepared up to a week in advance and are delicious spread on crostini or as an accompaniment to a simple roasted or grilled entrée.
✗ *Serves 4 to 6*

4 medium red bell peppers
¼ cup extra virgin olive oil
2 teaspoons capers, drained

4 anchovies, roughly chopped
6 fresh basil leaves, julienned

1] Roast the peppers according to the instructions on page 5. Slice the peppers into ½-inch-wide strips lengthwise.

2] Heat the olive oil in a medium skillet over moderate heat. Add the pepper strips, capers, and anchovies and sauté until the juices meld, 5 to 10 minutes. Transfer to a shallow ceramic or glass dish. Set aside to cool and serve at room temperature, garnished with the basil. Peppers can sit on a buffet up to 4 hours with no loss of flavor.

Italian Cooking for Beginners

ZUCCHINI PROSCIUTTO FRITTATA

Frittatas are the Italian equivalent of the French omelet. Unlike an omelet, however, frittatas can easily serve a large group, since they can be made up to 3 hours in advance and served at room temperature. They are perfect for informal gatherings. Always use a well-seasoned pan with an ovenproof handle. ✗ *Serves 6 as an appetizer or light lunch*

2 medium zucchini, skins on
6 ounces prosciutto, thinly sliced
8 jumbo eggs
¼ cup grated Parmesan cheese
2 tablespoons chopped fresh Italian
    parsley

¼ teaspoon coarse salt
¼ teaspoon white pepper
1 tablespoon olive oil
1 tablespoon unsalted butter

1] Trim the zucchini and coarsely grate with the food processor or hand grater. Cut the prosciutto or shred into ⅛-inch by 1-inch strips.

2] Beat the eggs with a fork in a large mixing bowl. Add the zucchini, prosciutto, Parmesan, parsley, salt, and pepper and combine with a fork. It is not necessary to beat this mixture too vigorously, since the purpose is to distribute the ingredients evenly, not to beat in air.

3] Preheat the broiler and position the rack about 6 inches from the heat. Heat the oil and butter in a medium skillet with ovenproof handle over medium-high heat. Pour the egg mixture into the pan and swirl to evenly set the bottom. Smooth the top with a fork.

After 1 minute, reduce the heat to medium-low and cook, uncovered, until the edges are set and the center runny, 10 to 14 minutes. Transfer to the heated broiler until the center is set and the top slightly golden, 1 to 2 minutes. Set aside to cool in the pan for 5 minutes.

To serve, run a dull knife along the inside edges to loosen. With a spatula, slide the frittata onto a round serving platter. Cut into wedges to serve either warm or at room temperature.

VARIATION. For potato and Parmesan frittata, first sauté in olive oil 1 medium onion and 1 large new potato, both thinly sliced. Add to the eggs along with ½ cup Parmesan and prepare as above.

CAPONATA

This sweet and sour eggplant relish is less astringent than that served in most restaurants. Caponata is a lovely spread to make ahead and bring to parties and picnics. It can be kept in the refrigerator up to 3 days, but return to room temperature before serving. Then add the toasted almonds and serve with crostini or plain crackers. ✖ *Serves 6*

1 large eggplant (about 1½ pounds), trimmed and cut into ½-inch cubes
Salt
4 celery ribs, trimmed and cut into ½-inch slices
½ cup red wine vinegar
⅓ cup currants
One 2½-ounce bag slivered almonds, for garnish

1½ cups plus 2 tablespoons olive oil
1 onion, peeled and chopped
½ cup large green olives, Italian or Greek, sliced off pit
⅓ cup capers, drained
2 tablespoons sugar
¼ cup tomato paste

1] Preheat the oven to 350 F. Place the eggplant cubes in a colander and sprinkle with salt. Set aside for about 45 minutes.

2] Bring a medium saucepan of water to a boil, add the celery, and cook at a rolling boil for 1 minute. Remove with a slotted spoon and reserve.

3] Combine the red wine vinegar and currants in a small bowl and set aside to plump.

4] Spread the almond slivers on a baking sheet and place in the oven, shaking occasionally, until evenly toasted, about 10 minutes. Turn off the oven and reserve the nuts.

5] After 45 minutes, pat the eggplant cubes dry with paper towels. Line the kitchen counters with a double layer of paper towels for draining. In a medium skillet over medium-high heat, heat 1½ cups of the olive oil. Fry the eggplant in batches until golden brown on all sides, being careful not to crowd the pan. Use a slotted spoon to turn the eggplant and remove from the pan. Drain on paper towels.

6] Heat the remaining 2 tablespoons of oil in another medium skillet over moderate heat. Cook the onion until soft but not brown, about 3 minutes. Add the blanched celery and cook an additional minute. Add the red wine vinegar and currants, olives, capers, sugar, and tomato paste.

Stir to combine, lower the heat, and simmer, uncovered, about 8 minutes. Add the fried eggplant and cook an additional 3 minutes.

7] Set aside to cool. Sprinkle with toasted almond slivers and serve at room temperature or slightly chilled. To serve as an appetizer, mound on plates lined with romaine or oak leaf lettuce, accompanied by thinly sliced, toasted baguettes or bruschetta.

COOL GREEN BEANS

This refreshing salad can be served as a side dish or as part of an antipasto selection. The mint brings out the beans' sweetness so they resemble sweet peas. You can chill the beans as much as 4 hours in advance, but add the dressing right before serving to avoid losing color and crunch. ✗ *Serves 6*

1 pound green beans
¼ cup extra virgin olive oil
¼ cup fresh lemon juice

3 tablespoons chopped fresh mint
¼ teaspoon salt
Freshly ground black pepper

1] Trim the beans and cut into 1-inch lengths diagonally.

2] Have ready a large mixing bowl of iced water. Bring a medium saucepan of salted water to a boil. Add the beans and cook 1 minute once the water returns to a boil. Drain in a colander and immediately transfer to iced water to stop the cooking. (This is called blanching.) Drain again, place the beans in a large bowl, and chill.

3] In a small bowl, whisk together the remaining ingredients. Immediately before serving, pour over the green beans, toss well, and serve.

GRILLED EGGPLANT
WITH SMOKED MOZZARELLA

Eggplant takes on a wonderful earthy flavor from the grill, enhanced here by smoky mozzarella and sweet balsamic vinegar.

✕ Serves 4

Olive oil
¼ cup extra virgin olive oil
2 tablespoons balsamic vinegar
2 teaspoons minced sun-dried
   tomatoes, packed in oil
½ teaspoon minced garlic, about
   1 small clove

Salt and freshly ground pepper
1 medium eggplant, skin on, stem
   removed
6 ounces smoked mozzarella

1] Preheat the grill or broiler, brushing the grate or broiler tray with olive oil.

2] In a small mixing bowl, combine extra virgin olive oil, balsamic vinegar, sun-dried tomatoes, and garlic. Whisk and season to taste with salt and pepper.

3] Cut the eggplant in about eight ¼-inch slices across the width and brush both sides of each slice with olive oil. Grill or broil one side until the edges turn black and grill marks appear, about 4 minutes.

4] Meanwhile, cut the smoked mozzarella into 8 slices. Turn the eggplant over, place a slice of cheese on each piece, and cook another 4 minutes, or until the cheese melts. If you are grilling outside, cover the grill to melt the cheese. Transfer to plates with spatula. Spoon the dressing over each and serve warm or at room temperature.

PASTA, RISOTTO, AND POLENTA

WHILE IT STILL MAY BE CONSIDERED UNPATRIOTIC IN ITALY TO SERVE A PLATEFUL OF PASTA, RISOTTO, OR POLENTA AS THE MAIN COURSE, HERE IN THE UNITED STATES WE HAVE ALWAYS KNOWN IT MAKES PERFECT SENSE TO FILL UP ON CARBOHYDRATES. NOW WE CAN EVEN FEEL VIRTUOUS WHILE DOING SO, SINCE NUTRITIONISTS TELL US IT IS HEALTHIER TO EAT A LARGE PORTION OF GRAINS ALONG WITH A BIT OF MEAT OR CHEESE. SO HEAP UP THOSE PASTA (OR RISOTTO AND POLENTA) BOWLS AND *MANGIA!* IT'S GOOD FOR YOU!

PASTA

After witnessing several great chefs produce the most ethereal strands of fresh pasta, only to have them solidify into a ball within moments of hitting the water, I do not recommend making pasta at home. The taste and texture of dry pasta is just as good or better. If it is physical therapy you are after in the kitchen, spend your time instead on an extravagant homemade dessert. Your efforts will be justly rewarded.

HOW TO COOK DRY PASTA

Nothing could be simpler. Bring a large quantity of water—4 quarts to a pound of pasta—to a boil in a large stockpot or pasta pot. When it comes to a vigorous boil, add 1 tablespoon of salt for flavor. If the salt is added earlier, a chemical reaction will slow down the time it takes to boil. Immerse the strands and keep them moving. Do not lower the heat. The water should remain at a continuous boil.

Check the pot intermittently and stir to prevent sticking. Ignore the times printed on the package and start testing for doneness after only a few minutes. Cooking time will vary according to the pasta's shape and thickness. Tiny orzo will be done in a minute or two, while hearty fettuccine may take as long as 15 minutes. To avoid mushy pasta, test often.

To test for doneness: Remove a strand and bite into it. When the center just loses its raw whiteness but the outside remains firm to the bite, it is al dente or "to the tooth." Tasting is the only accurate test. Throwing the pasta on a wall to see whether it sticks may be good for your pitching arm but it is not an accurate test.

A colander should be ready in the sink for draining. Immediately drain the pasta and do not rinse or add anything at this point. Quickly transfer the pasta to a bowl for tossing, or to the saucepan, according to the recipe. Toss well and serve.

SAUCING THE NOODLE

Most of the sauces in this and other cookbooks have been tested for a specific quantity of pasta, thereby begging the question of how much sauce to serve with the pasta. However, when in doubt, less is always best.

Too much sauce can drown the pasta, making it a limp and soggy soup, rather than the firm and substantial food it should be.

When you are unsure how much to use, start with the minimum—about 1 cup of sauce to a pound of pasta; toss and taste. Make small additions until the proportion is correct. Each strand should be generously coated, without a pool of liquid on the bottom of the bowl.

Pasta is best served in shallow bowls with a fork and spoon. Using a spoon to facilitate twirling is an Americanism, frowned upon in Italy, where the side of the bowl is deemed support enough for dangling strands. Most Americans, however, expect a spoon.

An intricate set of rules has evolved over the centuries for matching pasta with the correct sauces. Many of the authorities whose books are recommended on pages 110–112 offer specific guidelines.

Here are the Cliff Notes: Use long, thin strands like spaghettini with light tomato and oil-based sauces and seafood. Thicker noodles like fettuccine and linguine can support the more substantial cream, butter, and meat-based sauces, and funny shapes like farfalle or rotelle are good for catching crunchy bits of vegetable and meat or seafood. However, no one knows better than the Italians that rules are meant to be broken. Feel free to experiment and draw your own conclusions.

　Italian Cooking for Beginners

ANGEL'S HAIR PASTA WITH FRESH TOMATOES AND BASIL

Light cooking and a jolt of garlic bring out the sweet, fresh flavor of ripe tomatoes. Use dry pasta, either cappellini or the slightly thicker fedelini, and stay near the stove. Even dry, these thin shapes cook very quickly. ✗ *Serves 4 to 6*

3 tablespoons olive oil
4 garlic cloves, peeled and minced
1 small onion, peeled and diced
2½ pounds firm, large, ripe peeled tomatoes (see page 5), roughly chopped

½ teaspoon coarse salt
¼ teaspoon white pepper
½ cup chopped fresh basil
1 pound dry cappellini or fedelini
Grated Parmesan cheese

1] Bring a large pot of salted water to a boil for the pasta.

2] Heat the olive oil in a medium skillet or saucepan over medium-low heat. Cook the garlic with onion until soft and translucent, about 5 minutes. Add the tomatoes, salt, and pepper. Cook, uncovered, over moderate heat 15 minutes. Stir in the basil, cook 5 minutes more, and remove from heat.

3] Cook the pasta until al dente, 3 to 5 minutes for dry pasta. Drain in a colander. Transfer to a pasta bowl, top with the sauce, and toss well. Serve warm with Parmesan cheese for sprinkling.

Linguine with Bolognese Meat Sauce

One of those classic comfort foods that never goes out of style, *ragù,* as it is known in Italy, is the perfect topping for a flat pasta like linguine or tagliatelle, and also goes well with substantial shapes like farfalle or rotelle.

Preparation time is only 30 minutes, with an additional hour for simmering. *Serves 8*

2 tablespoons olive oil
2 tablespoons unsalted butter
1 onion, peeled and diced
1 carrot, peeled and diced
1 celery rib, diced
1 pound lean ground beef
½ pound lean ground pork
½ teaspoon salt
¼ teaspoon black pepper
1 cup dry red wine
One and a half 28-ounce cans Italian crushed tomatoes
1 bay leaf
¼ teaspoon nutmeg
½ cup whole milk
1½ pounds linguine or other wide pasta
Freshly grated Parmesan

1] Heat the olive oil and butter in a large heavy saucepan over low heat until the butter melts. Add the onion, carrot, and celery and cook until soft, about 10 minutes.

2] Add the beef, pork, salt, and pepper. Turn the heat to medium and cook, stirring frequently with a wooden spoon to crumble the meat and cook evenly. Cook until the meat loses its raw color.

3] Pour in the wine, turn up the heat, and boil until the liquid is absorbed. This is called reducing the liquid.

4] Add the tomatoes and bay leaf, reduce the heat to low, and simmer, uncovered, about 45 minutes or longer, whatever suits your taste and schedule. Remember to check the pot and stir occasionally to avoid scorching. (If you are in a hurry, partially cover the pot to speed things up.)

5] In about 45 minutes, when the sauce is nicely thickened, add the nutmeg to the milk and stir into the sauce. This mellows out the flavors by taming the tomatoes' acidity. Simmer while the pasta is boiling, or an additional 5 minutes if you are making it in advance.

6] Bring a large pot of salted water to a boil. Cook the pasta until al dente, drain in a colander, and transfer to a large pasta bowl. Pour on the sauce, toss well, and serve with Parmesan cheese for sprinkling.

PENNE ARRABBIATA

Arrabbiata is an uncomplicated tomato sauce flavored with red chile peppers. ✖ *Serves 4 to 6*

One 28-ounce can Italian peeled
  tomatoes
3 tablespoons olive oil
2 garlic cloves, peeled and minced
1 teaspoon red pepper flakes

Salt
2 tablespoons chopped fresh Italian
  parsley
1 pound penne

1] Bring a large quantity of salted water to a boil for the pasta.

2] Lift the tomatoes out of the can, reserving the liquid they are packed in. Holding them over the sink, gently squeeze to release the seeds. Roughly chop and reserve.

3] Heat the oil in a medium sauté pan over medium-low heat. Cook the garlic until its aroma is released but it remains white, about 3 minutes. Add the red pepper flakes and cook until the oil takes on some color from the pepper, 1 or 2 minutes.

Add the reserved tomatoes and their liquid. Bring to a boil, reduce to a simmer, and cook, uncovered, until thickened, about 15 minutes. Season to taste with salt and additional red pepper, if desired. Stir in the parsley and cook an additional 2 minutes.

4] Cook the pasta until al dente. Drain in a colander and transfer to a large serving bowl. Pour on the warm sauce, toss to combine, and serve immediately.

LINGUINE PUTTANESCA

Another robust tomato sauce, puttanesca sizzles with bits of garlic, anchovies, and olives. This easy version is adapted from Osteria Nonni, in Los Angeles. ✗ *Serves 4 to 6*

2 tablespoons olive oil
4 garlic cloves, peeled and thinly
  sliced
½ onion, peeled and sliced
One and a half 28-ounce cans
  Italian peeled tomatoes, seeded
  and finely chopped
½ cup Kalamata olives, sliced off
  the pit

6 anchovy fillets, or more to taste,
  chopped
2 tablespoons capers, drained
¼ teaspoon red pepper flakes
2 tablespoons chopped fresh Italian
  parsley or basil
1 pound linguine

1] Bring a large quantity of salted water to a boil.

2] Heat the olive oil in a medium sauté pan over moderate heat. Add the garlic and onion and cook until the onion is soft, about 5 minutes. Pour in the tomatoes and about half of the juice from the can. Turn up the heat and cook at a rapid bubble until slightly thickened, about 13 minutes. Reduce heat to medium-low and add the olives, anchovies, capers, and red pepper flakes. Cook, stirring occasionally, about 3 minutes more. Stir in the parsley or basil, cook 2 minutes more, and remove from heat.

3] Cook the linguine until al dente, drain in a colander, and transfer to a large serving bowl. Toss with the sauce and serve immediately.

Italian Cooking for Beginners

Linguine with Mediterranean Chicken and Artichokes

This light, healthy pasta sauce calls for many staples of the Italian pantry. *Serves 4*

3 boneless, skinless chicken breast halves
Salt and white pepper
3 tablespoons olive oil
2 garlic cloves, peeled and minced
One 6-ounce jar marinated artichoke hearts, drained and roughly chopped
½ cup Kalamata olives, sliced off the pit
3 large tomatoes, peeled, seeded, and diced
1 tablespoon plus 1 teaspoon capers, drained
Pinch red pepper flakes
2 tablespoons chopped fresh oregano, marjoram, or parsley
2 tablespoons canned chicken broth
1 pound linguine fini
Parmesan cheese (optional)

1] Set a large pot of water to boil.

2] Cut the chicken lengthwise into ½-inch-wide strips, then slice on the diagonal into ½-inch lengths. Lightly sprinkle with salt and pepper.

3] Heat 2 tablespoons of the olive oil in a medium skillet over high heat. Sauté the chicken until opaque, stirring frequently with a slotted spoon. Transfer to a bowl nearby.

4] Remove the pan from the heat for a couple of moments to cool it down and reduce the heat to low. With the pan back on the flame, add the remaining tablespoon of oil and the garlic. Cook until the aroma is released, about 2 minutes.

5] Add the artichokes and olives, turn the heat to medium, and cook, stirring frequently, about 3 minutes. Add the tomatoes, capers, red pepper flakes, and herbs and cook an additional 4 minutes to meld the flavors. Return the chicken to the pan along with the chicken broth and simmer about 4 minutes. (If your sauce is ready before the pasta, just reheat for a minute or two while the pasta is cooking.)

6] Salt the boiling water and cook the pasta until al dente. Drain in a colander and transfer to a large pasta bowl. Add the warm sauce to the pasta, toss well, and serve with Parmesan, if desired.

EGGPLANT LASAGNE

Lasagne is a wonderful, uncomplicated food for feeding a crowd. Although it takes some time to prepare, the technique is easy and you needn't make the entire recipe at one time. In this one, the fried eggplant slices can sit at room temperature while you refuel and the tomato sauce can be made a day ahead. ✗ *Serves 6 to 8*

2 medium eggplants, with skins
Salt
3 cups olive oil
3 sheets fresh egg pasta or ¾
    pound dry lasagne noodles

1 recipe Quick Tomato Sauce (see
    page 51)
1 pound fresh domestic mozzarella
    cheese, in water
1 cup grated Parmesan cheese

1] Trim the stems and end of the eggplant and cut into ¼-inch slices across the width. Sprinkle with salt on both sides and transfer to a colander to drain for 45 minutes. Pat dry with paper towels. (Salting is a necessary step. It removes excess bitterness and also makes the eggplant less absorbent—something you'll appreciate when you're frying.)

2] Line your kitchen counters with a double thickness of paper towels. Heat half the oil in each of two large skillets over high heat. If the amount of oil in this recipe makes you nervous, cut it in half and just use one pan. It will take twice as long but you won't have to think about all that oil.

It should take about 5 minutes to thoroughly heat the oil. Fry the eggplant in batches, until golden brown, 2 to 3 minutes per side. With tongs, transfer the eggplant to paper towels to drain and pat the tops dry. If you feel like taking a break, layer the eggplant on a large platter and cover with plastic wrap. It can be kept at room temperature up to 4 hours.

3] Prepare the tomato sauce.

4] Preheat the oven to 350 F. Coat the bottom of a 9 x 13 x 2-inch baking pan with a tablespoon or two of tomato sauce.

5] If you are using fresh sheets of pasta, they need not be precooked. Just trim them with a sharp paring knife to fit the pan. For dry pasta, cook the noodles in 4 quarts of rapidly boiling salted water until al dente. Drain, rinse with cold tap water, and set aside in a bowl of iced water.

6] The key to a good, light lasagne is to spread the ingredients evenly and to avoid double and triple thicknesses of noodles. Each bite should contain all of the flavors and you should never get a mouthful of just pasta. Begin assembling the lasagne with a layer of pasta. Top with an even layer of half the eggplant. Divide the tomato sauce into 3 parts, and spoon one part evenly over the eggplant. Top with half the mozzarella. Repeat the layers, ending with a layer of pasta and tomato sauce. Sprinkle the Parmesan over the top. Bake 45 minutes, or until golden brown and bubbly. Set aside to cool 10 minutes before slicing and serving.

LASAGNE-MAKING TIPS

☞ EVEN THOUGH THIS IS A CASSEROLE, SHOP FOR GOOD INGREDIENTS. IN THIS PARTICULAR VERSION, FRESH DOMESTIC MOZZARELLA AND FRESH PASTA WILL MAKE THE FINISHED DISH LIGHTER. IF YOU DO USE A HARD MOZZARELLA BE SURE TO GRATE, RATHER THAN CHOP, IT FOR BETTER MELTING.

AS FOR THE PASTA, FRESH IS ALWAYS PREFERABLE. MULTIPLE LAYERS OF DRY NOODLES CAN GROW THICK AND SOGGY IN THE PAN. FRESH NOODLES OR SHEETS ARE ACTUALLY FASTER TO COOK WITH, AS THEY DON'T NEED TO BE PRECOOKED. HOWEVER, IF YOU CAN'T FIND FRESH, TRY TO FIND *IMPORTED* DRY LASAGNE NOODLES SINCE THEY ARE THINNER THAN THE DOMESTIC VARIETY.

LINGUINE WITH BUTTER AND CHEESE

One of the simplest and most universally satisfying dressings for pasta. ✕ *Serves 2*

½ pound linguine
3 tablespoons unsalted butter,
   slightly softened

⅓ cup grated Parmesan cheese,
   plus additional for serving
Salt

1] Bring a large pot of salted water to a boil for the pasta.

2] Cut the butter into ½-tablespoon pieces and place 2 tablespoons in the bottom of the warmed pasta bowl.

3] Cook the pasta until al dente. Drain in a colander and transfer to the pasta bowl with butter. Toss well. Top with cheese and remaining butter and toss again. Season to taste with salt and serve warm with additional Parmesan for sprinkling.

SPAGHETTINI WITH OIL AND GARLIC

Here is the perfect dinner for one, along with a glass of wine and extra garlic, as desired. ✕ *Serves 2*

½ pound spaghettini or other thin
   pasta
⅓ cup olive oil
4 garlic cloves, peeled and minced
1 teaspoon salt

Pinch red pepper flakes
2 tablespoons chopped fresh
   arugula, parsley, or watercress
   for garnish (optional)

1] Bring a large pot of salted water to a boil for the pasta.

2] Meanwhile place the oil in a small saucepan with the garlic, salt, and red pepper flakes. Cook over low heat, swirling frequently, until the garlic's aroma is released and the color lightly golden. Do not let the garlic brown.

3] Cook the pasta until al dente. Drain in a colander and transfer to a serving bowl. Pour on the hot oil mixture and toss well. Sprinkle with greens, if desired, and serve immediately.

Farfalle with Asparagus and Prosciutto

This simple, elegant pasta dish based on a few well-chosen ingredients is the epitome of the pared-down Italian style. *Serves 4 to 6*

1 pound asparagus
Salt
6 ounces prosciutto, sliced twice as thick as paper
2 tablespoons unsalted butter
½ cup heavy cream
Freshly ground black pepper
1 pound farfalle or bow ties, or linguine
½ cup grated Parmesan cheese

1] Bring a large pot of salted water to a boil.

2] Wash and trim the asparagus by snapping off the hard, thick ends. Slice into 1-inch lengths along the diagonal. Fill a medium skillet with water 1 inch deep and bring to a boil. Salt the water and cook the asparagus until it can be easily pierced by a fork, 1 to 4 minutes depending on thickness. Drain in a colander, rinse with cold water to stop the cooking, and drain on paper towels. Wipe the skillet dry for later use.

3] Cut the prosciutto lengthwise into ½-inch-wide pieces and trim in half, along the length. Fluff to separate.

4] Melt the butter over moderate heat in the dry skillet. Sauté the prosciutto, stirring with a wooden spoon to separate the pieces, about 2 minutes. Be careful not to brown or crisp the meat.

5] Add the asparagus and cook, stirring frequently, just to heat through and coat with butter, about 2 minutes. Pour in the cream and season with a few grindings of pepper. Boil until the cream is reduced by half, about 4 minutes.

6] Meanwhile cook the pasta in the boiling water until al dente. Drain in a colander and transfer to a serving bowl. Toss with the warm sauce. Top with the ½ cup grated Parmesan and toss some more. Serve with additional Parmesan for sprinkling.

Penne with Garden Vegetables

Here is an easy primavera sauce, made with a minimum of fat.

Serves 4

10 ounces asparagus, hard ends trimmed and cut into 1-inch lengths
2 tablespoons unsalted butter
2 tablespoons olive oil
2 garlic cloves, peeled and minced
2 carrots, peeled and julienned
1 small zucchini, trimmed and julienned
1 small crookneck squash, trimmed and julienned
1 tablespoon chopped fresh thyme, or 1 teaspoon dried
2 tomatoes, peeled, seeded, and diced (see page 5)
Freshly squeezed lemon juice
Salt and pepper
1 pound penne
Parmesan cheese

1] Set a large pot of water up to boil.

2] Bring a medium saucepan or skillet of salted water to a boil. Blanch the asparagus until it can easily be pierced by a fork, 1 to 4 minutes. Drain in a colander, rinse with cold water, and reserve.

3] Heat the butter and oil in a 10-inch skillet over moderate heat. Sauté the asparagus, garlic, and carrots about 5 minutes, being careful not to brown the garlic.

4] Add the zucchini, crookneck squash, and thyme. Reduce heat to medium-low and cook, stirring occasionally, 10 minutes more. Stir in the tomatoes, season with lemon juice, salt and pepper to taste, and continue simmering until the flavors meld and the sauce thickens slightly, 5 to 8 minutes.

5] Salt the boiling water and cook the penne until al dente. Drain in a colander and transfer to a large pasta bowl. Top with the warm vegetable sauce and serve with Parmesan cheese for sprinkling.

SPAGHETTINI WITH SHRIMP AND GARLIC

Always purchase fish or shellfish from a busy fish market rather than the supermarket, if possible. Your chances are better of getting fish that has not been frozen or held on ice too long. Shrimp can be cleaned an hour or two in advance and reserved in a bowl, covered by a wet towel, in the refrigerator. ✗ *Serves 4 to 6*

1 pound medium shrimp
½ cup olive oil
3 garlic cloves, peeled and minced
¼ cup chopped fresh Italian
  parsley

¼ teaspoon red pepper flakes
1½ teaspoons salt
1 pound spaghettini

1] Set a large pot of water up to boil.

2] Meanwhile clean the shrimp by removing the shells with your fingers. With a paring knife, cut a ¼-inch slit along the center of the back and remove the black vein under cold running water. Don't be concerned if some shrimp don't have this black vein. They are safe to eat.

3] Heat the olive oil in a medium skillet over moderate heat. Sauté the garlic, 3 tablespoons of parsley, and the red pepper flakes until the garlic is soft but not brown. Add the shrimp and salt. Cook, stirring frequently, until the shrimp is pink all over, about 5 minutes. (If your pasta is not yet ready, keep the sauce warm on a very low flame.)

4] Meanwhile cook the pasta in salted water until al dente. Drain in a colander and transfer to a large serving bowl. Top with the warm shrimp sauce and toss well. Sprinkle with the remaining tablespoon of parsley and serve.

FUSILLI WITH BROCCOLI AND SUN-DRIED TOMATOES

Here is a good dish to serve when you are recovering from the previous night's excesses. While low in fat, it's high in fiber, so you won't feel deprived. ✂ *Serves 4 to 6*

3 bunches broccoli (about 1 to
   1¼ pounds)
¼ cup olive oil
4 garlic cloves, peeled and minced
¼ teaspoon red pepper flakes

1 teaspoon salt
3 tablespoons chopped sun-dried
   tomatoes packed in oil
1 pound fusilli
¾ cup Parmesan cheese

1] Trim the bottom inch and tough outer skins of the broccoli stalks with a sharp paring knife or vegetable peeler. Divide the florets from the stalks and thinly slice the stalks across the width into disks the width of a nickel. Trim florets into individual bite-sized pieces.

2] Bring a large saucepan of salted water to a boil and cook the broccoli for 1 minute after the water returns to a boil. Drain in a colander, rinse with cold tap water, and set aside to drain on paper towels. (The purpose of blanching—or rapid precooking in boiling water—is to slightly soften tough ingredients. Hard vegetables like broccoli, potatoes, and green beans are often blanched before being sautéed or roasted.)

3] Bring a large pot of salted water to a boil.

4] Meanwhile heat the oil in a medium sauté pan over moderate heat. Sauté the garlic until the aroma is released. Add the broccoli, red pepper flakes, and salt. Lower the heat and cook, stirring frequently, until the broccoli is evenly heated but still crisp, about 7 minutes. Stir in the sun-dried tomatoes and cook an additional 3 minutes.

5] Cook the pasta until al dente. Drain in a colander and transfer to the sauté pan with the broccoli mixture. With the heat turned low, toss to combine. Add the Parmesan, toss again, and serve. Pass additional grated Parmesan at the table.

Italian Cooking for Beginners

PENNE WITH OLIVES AND RICOTTA

Briny black olives and mild ricotta strike a lovely balance in this hearty uncooked sauce. For a casual summer lunch, try a sandwich of these two spreads with slices of tomato on toasted Italian bread. Black olive paste, also known as olivada, is also good by itself, spread on crostini. ✗ *Serves 4 to 6*

1 cup Kalamata or other good
    black olives
1 garlic clove, peeled
1 tablespoon capers, drained
2 tablespoons extra virgin olive oil
2 anchovies

Juice of 1 lemon
¼ cup chopped fresh basil
¾ cup ricotta cheese
2 roasted red peppers (see page 5)
1 pound penne or small ziti

1] Slice the olives off the pit. Combine olives, garlic, capers, olive oil, anchovies, lemon juice, and half the basil in a food processor fitted with the metal blade. Pulse until coarsely chopped and reserve.

2] In a small bowl, combine the remaining basil with ricotta and reserve.

3] Remove the stems and seeds of the roasted red peppers and cut into ½ x ¾-inch pieces.

4] Cook the pasta in a large quantity of salted water until al dente. Drain in a colander and transfer to a serving bowl. Add the reserved olive and ricotta mixtures. Toss well, scatter the red peppers over the top, and serve warm or at room temperature.

TOMATO SAUCE
MARINARA STYLE

Homemade sauce, even made with canned tomatoes, has a much cleaner, fresher flavor than any so-called "fresh" sauce sold in the bottle. Once you start making your own, you will be amazed at the over-powering flavor of salt in the commercial brands. Use this unfussy sauce on pizzas, long thin noodles, and as a topping for grilled eggplant or zucchini.

Marinara has a different meaning in Italy, where it is a tomato-based sauce with bits of seafood.

✂ Makes 3 cups, enough for 1 to 1½ pounds of pasta

2 tablespoons olive oil
2 garlic cloves, peeled and minced
2 small carrots, peeled and diced
2 small celery ribs, diced
1 medium onion, peeled and diced
1 tablespoon unsalted butter

One 28-ounce can crushed Italian tomatoes
2 bay leaves
2 teaspoons dried oregano
½ teaspoon coarse salt
Freshly ground black pepper
Pinch dried orange zest (optional)

1] Heat the oil in a medium heavy saucepan or dutch oven over moderate heat. Cook the garlic, carrots, celery, and onion until soft, about 10 minutes. Transfer to a food processor fitted with the metal blade and purée until a rough paste is formed.

2] Melt the butter in the same pan over moderate heat. Return the warm vegetable paste to the pan. Add tomatoes, bay leaves, oregano, salt, pepper, and orange zest if desired. Cook, stirring frequently, over low heat 15 minutes. The stirring is important to avoid scorching. Store in the refrigerator up to 5 days, or in the freezer 1 month.

VARIATIONS. For marinara with sausage, remove the meat from casings and sauté in a separate pan until just done. Add to the finished sauce and cook 5 minutes longer. For mushrooms, thinly slice ¼ pound white mushrooms and cook in the finished sauce an additional 10 minutes. Diced peppers can also be sautéed separately and stirred into the sauce as a flavoring. Marjoram, basil, or oregano are all good seasonings for tomato sauce.

QUICK TOMATO SAUCE

In the winter, when tomatoes taste like Styrofoam, I don't bother much with fresh tomato sauce. This recipe is enough for two pounds of pasta or one recipe of Eggplant Lasagne (see page 42).

✖ *Makes 5 cups*

¼ cup olive oil
2 garlic cloves, peeled and minced
1 medium onion, peeled and
    chopped
1 teaspoon salt
½ teaspoon white pepper

Two 28-ounce cans crushed
    Italian tomatoes
3 bay leaves
2 tablespoons chopped fresh basil
    or parsley

1] Heat the oil in a large saucepan over moderate heat. Cook the garlic and onion with salt and pepper until soft, about 10 minutes. Add the tomatoes and bay leaves. Bring to a boil, reduce to a simmer, and cook, uncovered, 15 minutes.

2] Stir in the basil, cook an additional 5 minutes, and remove from heat. Remove and discard bay leaves. This easy sauce may be kept in a covered container in the refrigerator up to 3 days.

CLASSIC PESTO SAUCE

Here is pure, unadulterated pesto sauce—perfect for warm pasta, minestrone soup, crostini, grilled fish, or stuffed chicken breasts. It keeps in the refrigerator about 4 days.

✖ *Makes 1 cup, enough for 1 pound of pasta*

2 bunches basil leaves (2 cups)
2 garlic cloves, peeled
2 tablespoons pine nuts
½ cup extra virgin olive oil

½ teaspoon coarse salt
½ cup grated Parmesan cheese

1] In a food processor fitted with the metal blade or a blender, combine basil, garlic, pine nuts, olive oil, and salt. Process until a smooth paste is formed. Scrape down the sides of the bowl once or twice to avoid huge chunks of garlic. Transfer the purée to a small mixing bowl.

2] Beat in the grated cheese with a spatula or wooden spoon. Store, covered, in the refrigerator up to 4 days. Before tossing with warm pasta, add a tablespoon or two of the pasta's cooking water, or if you wish a richer flavor, beat in 1 or 2 tablespoons unsalted butter.

3] To serve as pasta sauce, spoon pesto on hot pasta and toss to coat evenly. Serve with additional Parmesan for sprinkling.

Italian Cooking for Beginners

RISOTTO

Risotto is an easy dish to master. All it takes is a ladle, a wooden spoon, some patience, and a strong desire to eat well. The rest will fall into place with a little practice.

Always use Arborio rice, the short round grain from northern Italy, because it is more absorbent than other varieties. Cook risotto in a heavy-bottomed uncovered pot and stir constantly until the grains are soft on the outside but still a bit firm inside, about 20 minutes.

RISOTTO MILANESE

This is a great accompaniment to meats like Braised Short Ribs in Tomatoes (see page 75), and wonderful alone for a weeknight supper. If you have the time and inclination, by all means substitute fresh broth for the water and canned broth. ✕ *Serves 4*

One 14½-ounce can beef broth	⅛ teaspoon white pepper
2½ cups water	2 cups Arborio rice
5 tablespoons unsalted butter	½ cup dry white wine
1 onion, peeled and diced	Healthy pinch or 2 of saffron
¼ teaspoon salt	¾ cup grated Parmesan cheese

1] Combine the broth and water in a medium saucepan and heat to just beneath a boil.

2] Melt 3 tablespoons of the butter in a heavy large saucepan over medium-low heat. Cook the onion with salt and pepper until translucent. Add the rice, stirring occasionally to coat evenly with butter, and cook about 2 minutes. Add the wine, turn the heat to medium-high, and cook until the wine is nearly evaporated.

3] Here is where the rhythm changes—a chance to meditate or listen to music you love. Using a ladle, start adding the warm broth about ½ cup at a time, stirring constantly after each addition. Adjust the heat so the liquid in the risotto pot is always bubbling. Continue adding the broth, a ladle or two at a time, while constantly stirring. Make the next addition of broth when the rice grains have absorbed almost all of the previous addition, but never let the rice appear dry.

4] In a small bowl, set aside ½ cup of broth with the saffron and reserve.

5] When the rice is nearly done (after stirring about 20 minutes), add the saffron broth, stirring constantly until the rice is moist but al dente. Risotto should have a firm bite with no starchiness inside when done. If the rice needs additional liquid, add ¼ cup or so of water. Remove from heat.

6] Stir in the remaining butter and Parmesan cheese, combine well, and cover 5 to 10 minutes before serving. Pass additional Parmesan for sprinkling at the table.

Italian Cooking for Beginners

RISOTTO WITH DRIED PORCINI MUSHROOMS

When purchasing dried porcini look for large, light-colored pieces for the best flavor. Feel free to substitute other dried mushrooms like shiitake or chanterelles if they are more readily available.

✕ *Serves 6*

2 ounces dried porcini
    mushrooms, available at Italian
    markets and gourmet shops
4 cups lukewarm water
One 14½-ounce can beef broth
6 tablespoons (¾ stick) unsalted
    butter

1 onion, peeled and diced
1 garlic clove, peeled and minced
½ teaspoon salt
2 cups Arborio rice
½ cup dry red wine
¾ cup grated Parmesan

1] Soak the dried mushrooms in a bowl of the lukewarm water for 1 hour to reconstitute. Lift them out, saving the water, and feel for any tough bits of stem that may remain. Trim and discard. By hand, shred the mushrooms into large bite-sized pieces and reserve.

2] Pass the mushroom liquid through your finest strainer lined with a double layer of cheesecloth. If you don't stock cheesecloth, coffee filter paper is a good substitute. Discard any sand or twigs and reserve the soaking liquid for use in the broth.

3] Combine the soaking liquid with beef broth in a medium saucepan and bring to a low boil.

4] In a heavy medium saucepan, melt 4 tablespoons of the butter over medium-low heat. Cook the onion, garlic, and salt until vegetables are translucent, about 4 minutes. Add the rice, stirring to coat evenly with butter, and cook about 2 minutes. Pour in the wine and cook over moderate heat until it has nearly evaporated. Stir in the mushrooms and soon after that the first cup of the warm broth mixture.

5] Adjust the heat under the risotto so the liquid keeps bubbling and stir constantly, adding half a cup or so of broth just as the previous one is absorbed. It takes about 20 minutes of stirring to complete the dish.

6] When all of the liquid has been added or the rice is al dente, remove from heat. Stir in the remaining butter and Parmesan, cover, and let sit about 10 minutes before serving. Pass additional Parmesan at the table for sprinkling.

RISOTTO WITH ASPARAGUS

Saffron is very costly because of the time it takes to gather the stigmas of the saffron crocus by hand. Small vials or bottles of the threads are available in most good supermarket spice sections or by mail order. Avoid powdered saffron, since it lacks both the heady fragrance and the color of the real thing. ✖ *Serves 6*

12 ounces asparagus, washed and
 trimmed
One 14½-ounce can chicken
 broth
3 cups water reserved from
 asparagus
Salt (optional)

5 tablespoons unsalted butter
1 onion, peeled and diced
2 cups Arborio rice
½ cup dry white wine
Healthy pinch of saffron
¾ cup grated Parmesan

1] Slice the asparagus on the diagonal in ½-inch lengths. Bring a medium saucepan of salted water to a boil and blanch the asparagus about 2 minutes. Strain over a mixing bowl to retain the cooking water, and rinse the asparagus with cold water to stop the cooking. Reserve.

2] Combine 3 cups of the cooking water with chicken broth in a medium saucepan and bring to a near boil. Taste the liquid to see whether it needs additional salt. It needs character to add flavor to the rice, so add salt accordingly.

3] Melt 3 tablespoons of the butter in a heavy large saucepan over medium-low heat. Cook the onion until translucent. Add the rice, stirring occasionally to coat evenly with butter, and cook 2 minutes. Add the wine, turn the heat to medium-high, and cook until the wine has nearly evaporated.

4] Start adding the broth about ½ cup at a time, stirring constantly after each addition. The risotto pot should keep a constant boil. After about 10 minutes or once half the broth has been added, stir the asparagus into the risotto.

5] In a small bowl, combine ½ cup of the broth with the saffron and add to the risotto. Continue adding broth and stirring constantly until the rice is al dente. Add a tablespoon or so of hot water if the rice needs more liquid.

6] Stir in the remaining butter and Parmesan cheese. Cover and let rest 2 minutes before serving, with additional Parmesan for sprinkling.

POLENTA

Since it is such a plain starch, piping hot polenta is best served as an accompaniment to rich foods like Sausage and Tomatoes (see page 58). Leftover polenta can be shaped into loaves and refrigerated for later frying or grilling.

BASIC POLENTA

✖ *Makes 6 cups*

6 cups cold water
1 tablespoon salt

2 cups coarse cornmeal for polenta
2 tablespoons softened butter

1] Bring the water to a boil in a large heavy saucepan. Reduce to a simmer and add the salt. Measure the cornmeal into a bowl. Then add the cornmeal, drizzling it through your fingers a handful at a time, and stirring constantly with a wooden spoon. Continue stirring until the mixture holds together and pulls away from the sides of the pan, about 20 minutes. Turn off the heat and stir in the butter until melted. Serve piping hot.

2] If you wish to mold it for slicing, pour the hot cornmeal mixture onto a wooden board. Dip your hands in cold water and pat the hot polenta into a dome shape to cool. Slice when cool, or refrigerate.

VARIATION. For a richer version, substitute 1 cup milk for water. When polenta is done, stir in 2 tablespoons butter and ¼ cup grated Parmesan cheese.

POLENTA WITH
SAUSAGE AND TOMATOES

—————■—————

Serves 4

2 tablespoons olive oil
Salt
1 onion, peeled and roughly
    chopped
1 celery rib, diced

2 pounds sweet Italian sausage, cut
    in 2-inch lengths
1 cup crushed Italian tomatoes
Basic Polenta (see page 57)
Grated Parmesan cheese

1] Heat the oil in a large skillet over low heat. Add salt to the onion and celery and cook until soft, about 10 minutes.

2] Turn the heat to moderate and add the sausage pieces in one layer. Cook, stirring occasionally, until the meat loses its pink color, about 10 minutes. Pour in the tomatoes and cook, uncovered, about 20 minutes. It is important to stir frequently to avoid scorching.

3] Meanwhile, prepare the polenta. When it is nearly done, turn a bit of heat on under the sausages to rewarm. To serve, spoon the hot polenta onto 4 serving plates. Ladle on the sausages and tomato sauce. Serve warm with grated Parmesan cheese.

PIZZA

PIZZA-MAKING IS ONE OF THE REAL JOYS OF ITALIAN COOK-
ING. THIS SIMPLE YEAST DOUGH CAN BE MADE IN THE FOOD
PROCESSOR IN A MATTER OF MINUTES. HOWEVER, IF YOU
DON'T HAVE TIME FOR DOUGH-MAKING, TRY THE PREBAKED
BOBOLI PIZZA CRUSTS AND FOLLOW THE INSTRUCTIONS ON
THE PACKAGE. THEY ARE FASTER AND FRESHER-TASTING
THAN FROZEN DOUGH.

Pizza Dough

Makes 6 individual 8-inch pizzas or 5-ounce dough balls

About 1½ cups warm water
1 package (1 tablespoon) dry yeast
1 tablespoon sugar
3½ cups all-purpose flour
½ cup semolina or cornmeal
1 tablespoon salt
3 tablespoons olive oil

1] Fill a glass measuring cup with ½ cup of lukewarm tap water. Stir in the yeast and sugar and let stand until a head of foam appears at the top, about 10 minutes. (Proofing the yeast, as this is called, is a safeguard to see whether the yeast is still active. An expiration date stamped on the envelope gives you the life expectancy as well. If it doesn't foam, start the recipe again with new yeast.)

2] In a food processor fitted with the plastic dough blade, place flour, semolina or cornmeal, and salt. Pulse a few times to combine. Add the oil and process about 30 seconds.

3] With the machine running, add the yeast mixture through the feed tube. Gradually add the remaining water in a slow, steady stream until the dough clears the sides of the workbowl and forms a ball on top of the blade.

Since flour's absorbency varies according to climate and storage, the quantity of water in any bread recipe is a guideline. Keep an eye on the food processor and use more or less water as needed. As soon as the dough holds together and clears the sides of the bowl, enough water has been added. Once the ball forms, process an additional minute.

4] Lightly coat a large mixing bowl with olive oil. Remove the dough from the workbowl and shape into a smooth ball. Transfer to the mixing bowl, turning the dough a few times to coat all over with oil. Cover with a damp towel and set aside in a warm place to rest for about 20 minutes.

5] Lightly sprinkle a wooden board with flour. Turn the dough out and, with a knife, divide into 6 pieces. One at a time, punch down the dough balls and knead a few times. Form each into a ball and place on the board with 1 or 2 inches of space between. Cover with a damp towel and reserve again in a warm place for about 45 minutes, or until they increase in size about 20 percent. They are now ready for pizza-making. The dough balls can be wrapped well in plastic and stored in the refrigerator 1 day or in the freezer for 2 months. They will continue to rise slowly in the refrigerator.

Italian Rolls

Makes 6 rolls

Six 5-ounce pizza dough balls (see page 61)
Olive oil
Toppings such as coarse salt, chopped fresh rosemary, fennel seed, or sesame seeds

1] Preheat the oven to 425 F, with a pizza stone in place. If you do not have a stone, place the dough directly on an uncoated baking sheet before placing in the oven.

2] Brush the tops and sides with olive oil. Press on toppings and bake until the outside is golden and the center sounds hollow when flicked with a finger, about 20 minutes. Let cool 5 minutes.

3] Serve with extra virgin olive oil for dipping, or an Italian spreading cheese like ricotta (or even butter for a distinctively American touch).

Quick Pizza Sauce

Though not quite as fast as just opening a jar, making this sauce satisfies the need to digest as few preservatives as possible.

Makes enough sauce for four 8-inch pizzas

1 cup Italian peeled tomatoes, about 10 tomatoes, seeded and coarsely chopped
1 tablespoon tomato paste
2 teaspoons dried oregano
¼ teaspoon salt
¼ teaspoon white pepper

Combine all of the ingredients together in a small bowl.

PIZZA-MAKING TIPS

☞ To truly approximate the crisp, thin crust of restaurant pizza, use a pizza stone. Stones, or baker's tiles, also good for bread-baking, are available at cookware stores or by mail (see page 17). Make sure the stone you purchase can withstand 500 F heat.

Preheat the oven, with the stone in place for at least ½ hour. Before removing the stone for cleaning, let it cool off in the oven for a good long time.

Always spread a thin coating of liquid, either tomato sauce, olive oil, or whatever sauce you happen to be using, over the dough before adding the main ingredients. This coating will keep the main ingredients from sticking.

The purpose of the cheese is to melt and carry the flavors. If you want the cheese to be unobtrusive, use a mild mozzarella. Use more distinctive cheeses like fontina or goat cheese for a more pronounced flavor. Hard cheeses should always be grated for better melting.

PIZZA MARGHERITA

The classic tomato pizza. Refer to these master assembling and baking instructions for making other pizzas. ✂ *Serves 1*

Cornmeal
One 5-ounce pizza dough ball (see page 61)

2½ tablespoons Quick Pizza Sauce (see page 62)
½ cup grated mozzarella cheese

1] Preheat oven to 500 F, with a pizza stone or baking tray in place.

2] Sprinkle cornmeal on the pizza paddle and place a pizza ball on top. Force out the air by flattening with the palm of your hand. (If the dough is sticky, sprinkle a bit of flour on top.) With a lightly floured rolling pin, roll out the dough, making quarter turns to avoid sticking, until an 8-inch circle is formed. When rolling out the dough, work from the center to the outside and stop rolling a bit before you reach the outside edge. Resist the temptation to twirl it in the air.

Before you start assembling the toppings, slide the dough to the most forward edge of the paddle and lift the dough slightly. Sprinkle a little extra cornmeal between the dough and the paddle to ensure the pizza's gliding into the oven with one swift jerk.

3] Spread the tomato sauce in a thin layer over the dough, leaving about an inch bare around the edges for the crust.

4] Sprinkle the cheese over the sauce.

5] Now place the tip of the handle on the center of the hot stone at a slight upward angle and with a swift back and forth motion slide the pizza into the oven. Bake about 8 minutes, or until the crust is golden and the cheese bubbly. Remove with a spatula and place on a serving platter.

Italian Cooking for Beginners

PIZZA WITH ARUGULA, SAUSAGE, AND PARMESAN

This unusual combination comes from Trattoria Farfalle in Los Angeles. ✖ *Serves 1*

Cornmeal
One 5-ounce pizza dough ball (see page 61)
2½ tablespoons tomato sauce
⅓ cup grated mozzarella cheese
18 arugula leaves, stemmed and julienned

½ pound sweet Italian sausage
2 tablespoons grated Parmesan cheese
2 teaspoons chopped fresh basil

1] Preheat the oven to 500 F with a pizza stone in place.

2] Roll out the dough on a cornmeal-sprinkled paddle. Coat with tomato sauce, leaving the edges bare for crust.

3] Sprinkle on the mozzarella cheese and then arrange the arugula on top.

4] Remove the sausage from its casing and crumble over top. Top with Parmesan cheese and basil.

5] Bake 10 to 12 minutes, until the cheese melts and crust is golden. Serve immediately.

PIZZA WITH SAUSAGE, RICOTTA, AND SPINACH

✖ Serves 1

Cornmeal
One 5-ounce pizza dough ball (see page 61)
2½ tablespoons tomato sauce
¼ cup ricotta cheese
¼ cup plus 2 tablespoons (about 3 sprigs) fresh spinach leaves, washed, dried, and chopped

½ pound sweet Italian sausage
2 tablespoons grated Parmesan cheese

1] Preheat the oven to 500 F with a pizza stone in place.

2] Roll out the dough on a cornmeal-sprinkled pizza paddle. Spread on the tomato sauce, leaving edges bare for crust.

3] Spread the ricotta over the sauce, leaving 1 inch of tomato sauce uncovered along the outside. Scatter ¼ cup of the spinach over the top.

4] Remove sausage from its casing and crumble on top. Sprinkle with the remaining spinach and Parmesan and bake 10 to 12 minutes, until the cheese is bubbly and crust golden. Serve immediately.

POULTRY, MEAT, AND FISH

THE COMMON THEME OF THESE ENTRÉES IS THEIR EASE OF PREPARATION. NONE REQUIRES ADVANCE COOKING OR LENGTHY MARINATION TIME, AND WHILE THERE ARE SOME TRADITIONAL BRAISED DISHES HERE THAT REQUIRE SIMMERING FOR THEIR FLAVORS TO DEVELOP, THERE ARE NO TRICKY COOKING TECHNIQUES OR INTRICATE STEPS TO FOLLOW. MOST RELY ON THE CLASSIC ITALIAN FLAVOR COMBINATIONS AVAILABLE AT THE SUPERMARKET AND CAN BE PREPARED AN HOUR OR SO BEFORE DINNER IS TO BE SERVED.

ROASTED CHICKEN WITH LEMON AND ROSEMARY

You can simulate the restaurant technique of roasting chickens in a wood-burning oven by roasting at a very high temperature at home.

Rosemary and lemon are two classic Italian flavorings for poultry. Rosemary is considered such a natural enhancement that butchers in Italy often include a sprig along with the chicken. ✖ *Serves 4*

One 3½- to 4-pound chicken
1 garlic clove, peeled and crushed
Coarse salt
Freshly ground black pepper
2 large rosemary sprigs, or
   2 tablespoons dried rosemary

1 lemon, halved
4 tablespoons (½ stick) unsalted
   butter, softened

1] Wash the chicken with cold tap water and pat dry with paper towels.

2] Preheat oven to 475 F.

3] Rub the inside of the chicken's cavity with the garlic clove and sprinkle with salt and pepper. If using dried rosemary, rub it in the cavity, or stuff the cavity with fresh rosemary sprigs. Add the lemon halves. Tie the legs together with string and sprinkle the outside with salt and pepper.

4] With the chicken breast side up on the counter, loosen the breast skin with your fingertips. Insert half of the softened butter on each side of the breastbone and pat the skin to flatten and spread the butter. This will keep the bird moist.

5] Roast, uncovered, for 1 hour, or until the juices run clear when the bird is lifted. Baste every 20 minutes with the liquid in the pan. (If you don't have a basting or a pastry brush, tilt the pan and use a long-handled serving spoon to pour the juices over the top.)

6] Place bird on a cutting board and set aside to cool for 10 minutes. To carve, with a chef's knife or cleaver remove the wings and legs along the thighs. If the bird is large, split each leg at the joint between the thigh and drumstick. Divide the breast in half along the breast bone and pick off any remaining meat. Arrange on a platter and drizzle on the juices from the cutting board before bringing to the table.

FRICASSEE OF CHICKEN AND SAUSAGE

This homey casserole was inspired by Concetta Rinaldi. Be sure to spoon on the pan juices and serve with plenty of warm, crusty bread!
✖ *Serves 6*

2 pounds Italian sweet sausage
6 tablespoons olive oil
3 pounds chicken parts, (breasts, thighs, legs, and wings)
Salt and freshly ground pepper
1 medium onion, peeled and chopped
2 garlic cloves, peeled and minced

3 bell peppers, red, yellow, and green as available, cored, seeded, and cut in 1-inch squares
½ cup dry white wine
Juice of 1 lemon
2 tablespoons chopped fresh Italian parsley for garnish (optional)

1] Preheat the oven to 350 F.

2] Puncture each sausage a few times with a skewer. Heat 2 tablespoons of the oil in a large skillet over moderate heat. Cook the sausages, turning occasionally, until brown. Transfer to a platter lined with paper towels to cool and drain.

3] Wash and dry the chicken pieces and sprinkle with salt and pepper. Add 2 more tablespoons of oil to the skillet. Sauté the chicken pieces until brown all over. Transfer to an uncoated ovenproof casserole.

4] In another skillet, heat the remaining 2 tablespoons of oil over medium-low heat. Cook the onion and garlic with a sprinkling of salt until soft, about 10 minutes. Add the peppers and cook an additional 10 minutes.

5] Meanwhile slice each sausage into 2-inch lengths. Arrange the sausage pieces with the chicken in the casserole. Scatter the pepper and onion mixture on top. Drizzle with the wine.

6] Bake, uncovered, about 50 minutes. Remove from the oven and season with juice of 1 lemon. Garnish with the parsley, if desired, and let sit 10 minutes before serving.

OLD-FASHIONED
CHICKEN CACCIATORE

Chicken cacciatore, or hunter's style, is a great dish for informal winter gatherings. As with any stew, you can prepare it a day or two in advance with no loss of flavor. Refrigerate after simmering for 40 minutes and then add the mushrooms and parsley right before serving.

Serves 4

3⅓ pounds chicken parts (breasts, thighs, and legs as you wish)
Salt and freshly ground pepper
Paprika
¼ cup olive oil
2 garlic cloves, peeled and minced
1 medium onion, peeled and diced
4 medium celery ribs, diced
1 teaspoon coarse salt

½ cup dry white wine
One 28-ounce can crushed Italian tomatoes
2 teaspoons dried oregano
2 bay leaves
¼ teaspoon red pepper flakes
½ pound mushrooms, cleaned and thinly sliced
¼ cup chopped fresh Italian parsley

1] Wash the chicken and pat dry with paper towels. With a chef's knife or cleaver, cut each half breast in half again, across the width. Sprinkle chicken pieces all over with salt, pepper, and paprika.

2] Heat 3 tablespoons of the oil in a heavy dutch oven over medium-high heat. Being careful not to crowd the pan, brown the chicken in batches and transfer to a platter.

3] Add the remaining 1 tablespoon of oil to the pot and reduce the heat to medium-low. Cook the garlic, onion, and celery, adding salt, until the vegetables are soft and slightly golden, 10 minutes. Stir occasionally with a wooden spoon, scraping the bottom to release browned bits.

4] Pour in the wine, turn the heat to medium-high, and boil for 2 minutes. Then return the chicken to the pot along with the crushed tomatoes, oregano, bay leaves, and red pepper flakes. Stir well.

5] Bring to a boil, reduce to a simmer, and cook, covered, 40 minutes. Stir in the mushrooms and cook an additional 10 minutes without the cover. Then stir in the parsley and cook 5 minutes more. Serve in bowls over any medium-sized pasta such as penne, ziti, or farfalle.

Stuffed Chicken Breasts with Prosciutto

Boneless chicken breasts are a staple for week-night cooking. They can be sautéed, poached, grilled, broiled, or baked with any number of flavorings for a quick, healthy meal.

This quick chicken dish has the virtue of being easy but looking impressive. Serve it to guests with some crisp breadsticks, lightly cooked asparagus, and a chilled white wine. Nobody will know it took 20 minutes to prepare. *Serves 4*

¼ pound prosciutto, thinly sliced
4 boneless chicken breasts, skin on
Olive oil
Salt and white pepper
3 tablespoons unsalted butter
2 shallots, peeled and minced
¼ cup dry white wine
¼ cup chicken stock or canned broth
6 sprigs fresh thyme, leaves only, finely chopped

1] Preheat grill or broiler.

2] Divide the prosciutto into 4 equal portions. Stuff each breast by running a finger between skin and meat, leaving the skin attached on one side. Insert the prosciutto between skin and meat, being careful to cover the ham completely with skin.

3] On a work counter, cover the breasts with plastic wrap and press a heavy rolling pin over them to flatten slightly. A wine bottle or heavy glass will do if you don't have a pin. Remove the plastic and lightly coat the chicken all over with olive oil. Season with salt (lightly, since the prosciutto is salty) and pepper.

4] Broil, skin side up, 6 minutes per side. If you are doing this on the grill, cook with the skin toward the coals first.

5] Meanwhile make the sauce. In a medium skillet, melt 1 tablespoon of the butter over medium-low heat. Cook the shallots just until soft, about 2 minutes. Swirl in the wine, turn the heat up to medium, and reduce until only a light coating of liquid remains in the pan. Add the chicken stock and thyme and continue boiling until the liquid is reduced by half. Reduce the heat to low, break the remaining 2 tablespoons of butter into small pieces, and whisk them into the pan. Remove from heat as soon as the butter melts. Spoon the sauce over chicken breasts and serve.

GRILLED GAME HENS
WITH LEMON AND HERBS

This is one of my summertime favorites for entertaining large groups. Substitute poussin or quail if available. ✗ *Serves 4*

4 Cornish game hens, about
    12 ounces each
2 cups olive oil
1 tablespoon coarse salt
2 teaspoons cracked black pepper
½ cup fresh lemon juice
3 garlic cloves, peeled and crushed

2 cups roughly chopped mixed
    fresh herbs such as mint, basil,
    and parsley
Salt
Fresh herb sprigs and lemon
    wedges for garnish

1] Rinse the hens with cold water and remove the necks and giblets. Split in half along the length: Rest each breast side up on a work counter; with a heavy cleaver or chef's knife, split along the breastbone. Then flatten and with a few up-and-down whacks cut along the backbone. Trim any excess fat and skin. Dry the birds with paper towels.

2] In a large roasting pan, combine the olive oil, salt, pepper, lemon juice, garlic, and herbs. Add the hens and mix so the flavorings are evenly distributed. Cover with plastic wrap and set aside 3 hours at room temperature.

3] Preheat the grill or broiler. Cook, skin side toward the flame first, about 12 minutes per side. Sprinkle with salt to taste. If arranging a platter, garnish with fresh herb sprigs and lemon wedges and serve.

TURKEY SCALOPPINE
WITH LEMON AND PARSLEY

―――――――■―――――――

Turkey, now available cut in parts in the supermarket, makes a good substitute for the more expensive and less flavorful veal traditionally served this way. You can make a quick week-night dinner by serving turkey breast alongside some simple greens such as Broccoli with Garlic (see page 93) or Spinach Sauté (see page 96) and some crusty Italian bread. ✖ *Serves 4*

1½ to 2 pounds turkey breast
    slices, ⅛ inch thick
¼ cup all-purpose flour
½ teaspoon salt
¼ teaspoon white pepper
3 tablespoons olive oil
3 tablespoons cold unsalted butter

1 shallot, peeled and minced
¼ cup dry white wine
1 teaspoon capers
Juice of 1 medium lemon
2 tablespoons chopped fresh Italian
    parsley

1] Preheat the oven to 200 F. Wash the turkey slices and arrange between 2 sheets of plastic wrap on a countertop. Pound to flatten with a mallet, rolling pin, or heavy glass.

2] Combine the flour, salt, and pepper on a large platter. Dip each turkey slice to coat and pat off any excess flour.

3] Heat the olive oil in a medium skillet over medium-high heat. Sauté the turkey, 2 or 3 slices at a time, about 1 minute per side. When the edges turn white, turn the meat over. Transfer the finished slices to an ovenproof platter and when all are done, reserve in the warm oven.

4] Remove the pan from heat to cool for a minute or two. Reduce the heat to low and return the pan. Melt 1 tablespoon of the butter and cook the shallots for 1 minute. Turn up the heat and pour in the wine, scraping the bottom of the pan with a wooden spoon to loosen any browned bits. Boil until the wine is nearly evaporated. Reduce the heat to low. Then add the capers, lemon juice, and parsley and simmer an additional 2 minutes. Break the remaining 2 tablespoons of cold butter into several pieces and stir into the sauce. As soon as the butter melts, remove from heat.

5] Arrange turkey slices on serving plates, spoon on the sauce, and serve.

BRAISED SHORT RIBS
IN TOMATOES

■

This rustic dish comes from my friend Michael Villella of Los Angeles. He learned it from his mother, Teresa, who like other Italian immigrants of her generation, was expert at taking inexpensive ingredients and revealing their deep, rich flavors by slow cooking. The results are similar to ossobuco, in that the bones and their connective tissue make a rich sauce in the pot. Braised short ribs make a wonderful Sunday night supper with a side course of Risotto Milanese (see page 53). ✖ *Serves 4 to 6*

¼ cup all-purpose flour
2 teaspoons salt
½ teaspoon white pepper
¼ teaspoon cayenne
4½ pounds beef short ribs
½ cup olive oil
2 garlic cloves, peeled and minced
1 onion, peeled and finely
    chopped
2 celery ribs, finely chopped

1 carrot, finely chopped
One 28-ounce can Italian crushed
    tomatoes
1 cup water
2 tablespoons tomato paste
1 tablespoon dried oregano
1 bay leaf
Salt and pepper
¼ teaspoon red pepper flakes

1] Combine the flour, salt, white pepper, and cayenne on a large platter. Dip the short ribs in the mixture to coat lightly on all sides, and set aside. To remove excess flour, pat the ribs briskly with your hands.

2] Heat the olive oil in a large, heavy dutch oven over medium-high heat. Brown the ribs on all sides, in batches if necessary, and transfer to a platter. Pour off and discard about half of the fat in the pan.

3] Reduce the heat to low, add the garlic, onion, celery, and carrot and cook until nearly golden, about 10 minutes. Occasionally scrape and stir the bottom of the pan with a wooden spoon to loosen any browned bits of meat.

4] Pour in the crushed tomatoes, water, tomato paste, oregano, bay leaf, and remaining seasonings. Turn the heat to medium-high and bring the sauce to a boil. Add the browned ribs, reduce heat to low, and simmer, covered, about 3 hours. Check the pot and stir occasionally to prevent scorching.

When done, the meat should fall off the bone when gently scraped with a wooden spoon or fork. This type of dish can be cooked longer or shorter depending on your taste and schedule—nothing fussy about it. It also benefits from spending a day or two in the refrigerator.

5] Before serving, lift the meat out with a slotted spoon or tongs and place on a platter. With a ladle skim off and discard any fat that has risen to the top. Spoon the remaining sauce over the meat and serve alongside Risotto Milanese or over a bed of pasta such as penne. If you happen to have a dog in the house, give him a warm bone. You'll make a friend for life.

ITALIAN-STYLE MEATLOAF

━━━━━━━━■━━━━━━━━

This Italian meatloaf, made with all fresh ingredients, is exceptionally tender and moist. The optional sauce makes it special for guests, but feel free to serve it with ketchup to the family. ✖ *Serves 6*

2 tablespoons unsalted butter
3 garlic cloves, peeled and minced
1 onion, peeled and diced
2 celery stalks, chopped
3 tablespoons chopped fresh rosemary or any combination of parsley, sage, mint, oregano, and marjoram
¼ cup pine nuts

1 pound ground veal
½ pound ground beef
½ pound ground pork
2 eggs, beaten
¾ cup fresh bread crumbs
1 teaspoon fennel seeds, crushed
2 teaspoons salt
1 teaspoon white pepper

1] Preheat oven to 350 F.

2] Melt the butter in a medium sauté pan over moderate heat. Cook the garlic, onion, celery, and herbs just until soft, 10 to 15 minutes. Set aside to cool.

3] Spread the pine nuts on a baking sheet and toast in the preheated oven until golden, about 10 minutes. Shake the pan occasionally to ensure even cooking.

4] Combine the ground meats in a large mixing bowl, using a fork to break up and toss the ingredients. Add the remaining ingredients and the warm onion and herb mixture. Mix well with a wooden spoon and loosely pack into a 9 x 5 x 3-inch loaf pan.

5] Bake, uncovered, 50 to 60 minutes, or until the top is slightly browned and the edges pull away from the sides of the pan. Set aside to cool for 10 minutes. Drain and discard any liquid in the pan. Cut in slices and serve with Roasted Red Pepper Sauce (recipe follows).

ROASTED RED PEPPER SAUCE

Makes 1½ cups

2 red bell peppers, roasted, peeled, seeded, and roughly chopped (see page 5)
1 tomato, peeled, seeded, and diced

2 tablespoons extra virgin olive oil
Salt, pepper, and Tabasco

1] Combine the peppers and tomato in the blender or food processor and purée.

2] Heat the olive oil in a small skillet over high heat. Pour in the puréed peppers and tomatoes and season to taste. Cook at a rapid boil for 3 minutes and serve warm.

STEAK PIZZAIOLA WITH PEPPERS AND ONION

Italian sauces are more often an amalgamation of cooking liquids concentrated in the pan than an afterthought to be created separately. This natural style is the outcome of a cuisine that respects home cooking as much or more than restaurant cooking. Leftovers are great reheated and served on crusty Italian rolls. ✖ *Serves 4*

3 tablespoons olive oil
1 onion, peeled and sliced
1 teaspoon coarse salt
1 red bell pepper, cored, seeded, and sliced
1 green bell pepper, cored, seeded, and sliced

1½ pounds flank steak
Salt and freshly ground pepper
1 cup Italian tomato purée
½ cup cold water
1 tablespoon dried oregano

1] Preheat the oven to 350 F.

2] Heat the olive oil in a dutch oven over medium-low heat. Cook the onion with coarse salt until the onion begins to soften, about 3 minutes. Add the red and green pepper and cook over moderate heat, stirring occasionally, 8 minutes.

3] With a chef's knife, score the steak intermittently on both sides to prevent curling. Season with salt and pepper. Place the steak over the bed of peppers and onion. Top with the remaining ingredients, cover, and transfer to the oven.

4] Bake 1 hour with the lid on, turning the meat after ½ hour. Remove the lid and return to the oven for 15 to 30 minutes, until the sauce is thickened to your taste.

5] Remove from oven. Place the meat on a cutting board to cool 10 minutes. Then slice thinly on the diagonal, across the grain. If serving immediately, arrange the slices on serving plates and spoon on the sauce. If serving later, return the sliced meat to the pot and let it soak up the sauces until serving time. Reheat over a low flame, if necessary.

BRAISED VEAL SHANKS
WITH PEAS

Shank has such a full flavor that I prefer this simple preparation to the heavier ossobuco. ✘ *Serves 4*

¼ cup flour
Eight 1-inch slices hind veal
   shanks
4 tablespoons (½ stick) unsalted
   butter
2 tablespoons olive oil

Salt and freshly ground pepper
2 cups dry white wine
2 sprigs fresh rosemary
¼ cup water
½ pound sugar snap peas, shelled
1 tablespoon fresh lemon juice

1] Place the flour in a bowl and dip the shanks to lightly coat.

2] Melt 2 tablespoons of the butter and the oil over medium-high heat in a skillet large enough to hold the meat in one layer. Brown the shanks on both sides and then season with salt and pepper.

3] Add the wine, rosemary, and additional salt and pepper. Reduce the heat to low. Cover and cook, turning occasionally, until the meat begins to fall off the bone, about 1½ hours.

4] Remove the shanks and reserve on a platter. Remove and discard the rosemary sprigs. Add the water, turn up the heat, and boil for a minute, scraping the bottom of the pan to release browned bits. Add the peas and cook an additional 2 minutes. Turn off the heat. Stir in the remaining 2 tablespoons of butter until melted and then stir in the lemon juice. Adjust seasonings with salt and pepper. Spoon the sauce over the meat and serve immediately.

VEAL BUNDLES WITH FONTINA AND SAGE

Ask the butcher for slices from the top round, as they are more flavorful and large enough to roll round and enclose the filling. Serve this elegant main course with a simple vegetable dish like Spinach Sauté (see page 96). *Serves 4*

⅓ cup all-purpose flour
½ teaspoon salt
¼ teaspoon white pepper
2 eggs, lightly beaten
½ cup fine dry bread crumbs (see page 9)
8 slices (about 1 pound) veal scaloppine, top round
24 large fresh sage leaves, stems removed
½ pound grated fontina cheese
2 tablespoons vegetable oil
5 tablespoons unsalted butter
1 tablespoon chopped fresh sage

1] Combine the flour, salt, and pepper with a fork in a small shallow bowl. In 2 other bowls nearby arrange the beaten eggs and bread crumbs.

2] Wrap the veal in plastic wrap and flatten with a mallet or rolling pin to about ⅛-inch thickness.

3] Lay the veal slices on a work counter. Place 3 sage leaves across the width of each, diagonally. Divide the cheese and sprinkle it evenly over the sage, leaving the edges of meat uncoated. Roll each, beginning at the narrow end, along the width, to form a small, tight cylinder. Fold over the edges to seal the ends and enclose the filling.

4] One at a time, dip each roll first in the flour to lightly coat. Pat with your hands to remove excess flour. Then dip in the eggs, holding the roll over the bowl a moment to drain, and roll in the bread crumbs to coat. Reserve on a plate in the refrigerator at least ½ hour or up to 2 hours to set.

5] Preheat the oven to 350 F.

6] Heat the oil and 2 tablespoons of the butter in a large ovenproof skillet over medium-high heat. Sauté the chilled veal rolls until brown on all sides. Transfer to the oven and bake until the cheese begins to ooze, about 7 minutes.

7] Meanwhile melt the remaining 3 tablespoons of butter in a small pan over low heat. Add the chopped sage and cook about 2 minutes. Transfer the finished veal to plates and spoon on the warm butter and sage. Serve at once.

GRILLED VEAL CHOPS
WITH ROSEMARY

This is the type of simple dish to serve in the summertime when, if you grill some vegetables, you can cook the entire meal outdoors.
You can toss some rosemary sprigs from the marinade onto the charcoal for wonderfully scented chops. ✕ *Serves 4*

8 garlic cloves, peeled and crushed   1 cup olive oil
8 sprigs fresh rosemary   Salt and pepper
Four 12-ounce veal loin chops   Lemon wedges for garnish

1] Place 4 of the garlic cloves and 4 sprigs of rosemary in a dish for marinating. Place the chops over the garlic and rosemary. Top each chop with 1 clove of garlic and a rosemary sprig. Pour the oil over all. Cover with plastic wrap and refrigerate 8 to 48 hours.

2] Remove the chops from refrigerator about 1 hour before serving. Prepare the grill and let the flames subside some. Veal is best cooked over moderate coals. Grill the chops about 5 minutes per side. Sprinkle with salt and pepper at the table and serve with lemon wedges.

VEAL CUTLETS MILANESE

These are cutlets prepared the traditional northern Italian way—simply breaded and fried. They are also delicious topped with a tablespoon or two of marinara sauce, fresh chopped tomatoes, or layered in sandwiches with roasted peppers or eggplant. ✖ *Serves 4*

8 slices (about 1 pound) veal
   scaloppine, top round
¼ cup flour
2 eggs
1 cup fine dry bread crumbs

¼ cup grated Parmesan cheese
3 tablespoons unsalted butter
2 tablespoons olive oil
Salt
Lemon wedges for garnish

1] Place the veal between sheets of plastic wrap and pound with a mallet to flatten.

2] Arrange the flour, eggs, and bread crumbs each in their own shallow bowl. Mix the eggs with a fork. Add the Parmesan cheese to the bread crumbs and combine with your fingers.

3] Dip each cutlet first in the flour. Pat off the excess and dip in the egg. Then dip in the bread crumb mixture, patting on the crumbs so the coating is even.

4] In a large skillet, melt the butter and oil over medium-high heat. Without crowding the pan, fry each cutlet until brown on each side, about 1 or 2 minutes per side. Transfer to a platter and sprinkle with salt. Garnish with lemon wedges and serve hot.

PORK TENDERLOIN WITH FENNEL CRUST

━━━━━■━━━━━

Lean tenderloin meat is coated with a savory crust in this quick version of the traditional Tuscan pork roast, *arista*. Be sure not to slice the meat too thinly or the delicious crust will get lost on the cutting board. Since the flavors are strong, serve along with a mild side dish like Roasted Potatoes with Sage (see page 97). An electric minichopper, if you happen to have one, is excellent for grinding the seasonings.

✂ *Serves 4*

1½ pounds pork tenderloin
4 garlic cloves, peeled and minced
1 tablespoon ground fennel seeds
1 tablespoon minced fresh
　rosemary

1½ teaspoons coarse salt
½ teaspoon cracked black pepper
⅓ cup olive oil

1] Preheat the oven to 450 F.

2] In a small mixing bowl, combine the garlic, fennel, rosemary, salt, pepper, and olive oil. Mix well with a fork.

3] Wash and pay dry the pork tenderloin. Place on a platter and brush all over with the olive oil mixture. The pork should be generously covered. Set aside at room temperature while the oven heats well, about 20 minutes.

4] Transfer the meat to a rack in a roasting pan and bake, uncovered, ¾ hour. Let cool for 10 minutes, and slice along the diagonal in ¼-inch slices. Again, if you slice the meat too thinly you'll miss your dollop of crust with each bite. Pour any juices from the cutting board on the meat and serve warm.

SAUSAGE AND PEPPERS

———————— ■ ————————

For a complete meal, serve this traditional favorite on a bed of plain pasta or polenta or on crusty Italian rolls as a sandwich. ✖ *Serves 4*

2 pounds Italian sausages, sweet
   or hot
¼ cup olive oil
1 garlic clove, peeled and minced
2 onions, peeled and thinly sliced
4 bell peppers, red or green, cored,
   seeded, and sliced

¼ cup dry white wine
½ teaspoon dried oregano
¼ teaspoon salt
Freshly ground black pepper

1] Puncture the sausages a few times with a skewer. Heat 2 tablespoons of the oil in a skillet over medium-low heat. Cook the sausages, turning occasionally, until lightly browned all over. Remove with tongs and drain on paper towels.

2] Add the remaining oil to the pan and cook the garlic and onions until slightly softened. Add the peppers, turn the heat to medium, and cook, stirring occasionally, about 15 minutes.

3] When the peppers have softened, pour in the wine and boil until reduced by half. Return the sausages to the pan along with oregano, salt, and pepper. Reduce the heat to low and cook, covered, about 20 minutes. To serve, place 2 sausages on each plate. Spoon on the pepper sauce and serve with plenty of bread.

LAMB STEW WITH
GREEN OLIVES AND LEMON

As with other braised dishes, this robust stew improves with a day or two in the refrigerator. Lamb shoulder meat is ideal for stews and braised dishes, and it is easy to find, cut in slices, in the supermarket meat case. ✕ *Serves 4*

3 pounds lamb shoulder, cut in 2-inch cubes, with small bones in
Salt and freshly ground black pepper
⅓ cup olive oil
2 garlic cloves, peeled and minced
1 cup dry white wine
1½ cups canned peeled tomatoes, seeds removed, roughly chopped

2 tablespoons chopped fresh oregano, or 1 tablespoon dried
1 cup or one 5-ounce jar good, unstuffed green olives such as Santa Barbara country-style or garlic-flavored
1 teaspoon grated lemon zest (from about 1 lemon)

1] Trim the lamb of excess fat. Generously season all over with salt and pepper. Heat the oil in a heavy dutch oven over medium-high heat. Brown the lamb in batches and reserve on a platter.

2] Pour off the fat, leaving about 2 tablespoons to coat the bottom of the pan. Reduce the heat to low and cook the garlic about 1 minute. Pour in the wine, chopped tomatoes, and dried oregano (if you are using fresh oregano, do not add until step 4) and return the lamb to the pot. Bring to a simmer and cook, covered, 1 hour. Check the pot and stir occasionally to avoid scorching.

3] Meanwhile bring a small pan of water to a boil and blanch the olives 2 minutes. Rinse with cold water and slice off the pit.

4] Add the blanched olives, fresh oregano, and lemon zest to the pot and simmer 30 minutes more, without the cover. Taste the meat. When it is buttery soft and flakes with a fork it is done. Continue cooking and checking the pot every 15 minutes or so until done to your liking.

5] Serve in bowls over a bed of pasta or rice. Or, for a more elegant presentation, lift the meat out with a slotted spoon and transfer to dinner plates. Spoon the juices judiciously over the top and serve with a starchy accompaniment such as roasted potatoes.

UPDATED SCAMPI

———————■———————

This updated, ten-minute version of scampi virtually eliminates the possibility of drying out and toughening the shrimp. It makes an elegant dinner served with steamed or Italian-style Mixed Grilled Vegetables with Balsamic Vinegar (see page 100). ✕ *Serves 4*

Olive oil
16 jumbo shrimp, about 1 pound, in the shell
Salt and pepper
8 tablespoons (1 stick) unsalted butter

4 garlic gloves, peeled and minced
2 tablespoons dry white wine
1½ tablespoons chopped fresh parsley or chives

1] Preheat the broiler and coat the broiler rack with olive oil.

2] Wash and pat dry the shrimp with paper towels. Butterfly, leaving the shells on, by slicing them open along the inside curve. Arrange on the broiler shell side up. Brush with olive oil and sprinkle with salt and pepper. Broil, one side only, 4 minutes.

3] Meanwhile melt the butter in a large skillet over medium-low heat. Cook the garlic and ¼ teaspoon salt until garlic is soft, about 3 minutes. Add the wine and simmer an additional 2 minutes. Transfer the shrimp to the pan, along with the parsley or chives, and toss with the butter sauce for a minute or two. Serve hot.

MUSSELS IN BROTH
WITH GARLIC AND PARSLEY

―――――■―――――

Most of the mussels sold at the market today are farm-raised and so do not require the multiple washings and purgings described in older cookbooks. Just rinse them under cold running water, remove their beards, and they are ready. ✗ *Serves 4*

50 mussels
¼ cup extra virgin olive oil
4 to 6 garlic cloves, peeled and
  minced
½ small celery rib, finely diced

½ cup chopped fresh Italian
  parsley
1½ cups dry white wine
Salt

1] To clean the mussels, scrub with a brush under cold running water. (A new toothbrush will do if you don't have a kitchen brush.) Remove any threads, or beard, clinging to the sides or center by yanking them off by hand. Place clean mussels in a large mixing bowl, cover with a wet towel, and reserve in the refrigerator.

2] In a large stockpot or pasta pot, heat the olive oil over medium-low heat. Cook the garlic, celery, and parsley until soft, about 5 minutes. Pour in the wine, bring to a boil, and cook 6 minutes.

3] Add the mussels, cover the pot, and shake it occasionally to distribute the wine and mussels evenly. Reduce the heat to medium and cook, covered, 10 minutes. Remove from heat.

4] Check the pot and remove and discard any closed mussels or open, empty shells. Taste the broth and salt it as needed. With a slotted spoon place a dozen or so mussels in each bowl and then ladle on the broth. Serve hot with bread for the juices.

BAKED TROUT WITH SPINACH AND PINE NUTS

———■———

The Italian way with fish is to cook it simply, allowing its natural goodness to shine through. In this presentation, chunks of garlic and toasted pine nuts in a spinach base add interest without diminishing or overpowering the moist, flavorful meat. At the store, ask them to completely bone and scale the fish, leaving the heads and tails on for a nice presentation. Any whole white fish may be substituted. ✖ *Serves 4*

¼ cup pine nuts
3 large garlic cloves, peeled
1 tablespoon unsalted butter
1 bunch spinach, washed, stems
    trimmed, and roughly chopped
Salt and white pepper

Four 6- to 8-ounce trout, bones
    and scales removed, with heads
    and tails on
Olive oil
Lemon wedges for garnish

1] Preheat the oven to 325 F.

2] To make the stuffing: Arrange the pine nuts on a baking sheet and toast in the warm oven, shaking the pan occasionally, until golden brown, about 4 minutes. Turn the oven up to 350 F.

Bring a small saucepan of water to a boil and blanch the garlic 3 minutes. Rinse in cold water and roughly chop in large chunks.

Melt the butter in a medium saucepan over medium-high heat. Cook the spinach with a pinch of salt, stirring frequently, until wilted and bright green, about 2 minutes.

Squeezing out any excess liquid, transfer the spinach to a bowl. Add the garlic and pine nuts; mix and reserve.

3] Divide the spinach stuffing into 4 equal portions. Lay each fish on the counter, belly up, and sprinkle the inside with salt and pepper. Evenly spread the filling along one side of each and cover with the other side. Brush the outside with olive oil and sprinkle with salt and pepper.

4] Place each trout in the center of a 9-inch-long piece of aluminum foil. Fold over to enclose the fish, pressing out excess air. Seal the packet by crimping the edges tightly around the fish.

5] Place packets on baking tray and bake 20 minutes. The packets will puff when done. To serve, cut packets open with a knife. With a spatula transfer fish to four serving plates and pour the juices from the packet over them. Garnish with lemon wedges and serve warm.

SWORDFISH SKEWERS WITH PEPPERS AND LEMON

Grilled swordfish is a favorite in southern Italy, where the best fish is caught in the Straits of Messina, between Sicily and Calabria. This healthy, light combination refreshes both the eyes and the palate with its bold colors and bright, clean flavors. ✕ *Serves 6*

2 pounds swordfish, cut about 1½ inches thick

MARINADE
½ cup olive oil
⅓ cup fresh lemon juice
1 teaspoon cracked black pepper
½ cup chopped fresh oregano or marjoram

1 yellow bell pepper, cored and seeded
2 red bell peppers, cored and seeded
½ red onion, peeled
3 small lemons
Salt
¼ cup fresh dry bread crumbs

1] If using bamboo skewers, soak 6 in water for 30 minutes and then place in the freezer before beginning. This will keep the wood from burning and splintering on the grill.

2] Remove any skin and cut the swordfish into 1½-inch cubes. Combine the marinade ingredients in a shallow ceramic or glass container and add the swordfish. Cover with plastic wrap and refrigerate 30 minutes, turning the pieces occasionally.

3] Preheat the grill or broiler and coat the grate with oil.

4] While the grill is heating, cut the peppers into 1-inch squares and cut the onion in 3 wedges. Halve the lemons across the width and then cut in 12 small wedges.

5] Assemble the skewers by alternating pieces of fish with 2 kinds of pepper, beginning and ending each with a sturdy wedge of lemon. Separate the onion into 6 pieces and place one in the center of each skewer. Sprinkle all over with salt and brush with the marinade.

6] Scatter the bread crumbs on a plate. Dip each skewer in crumbs to coat lightly.

7] Grill or broil until the fish turns opaque and the vegetables are charred on the edges, about 10 minutes total. Using tongs and a pot holder, turn the skewers every few minutes to cook evenly. Serve warm.

GRILLED TUNA WITH SALMORIGLIO SAUCE

This simple classic is from Sicily, source of the best tuna and swordfish in Italy. The sauce is delicious with either fish. ✗ *Serves 4*

Olive oil
¼ cup extra virgin olive oil
2 tablespoons lemon juice
1 tablespoon chopped fresh
  oregano

½ tablespoon salt
· Freshly ground black pepper
Four 6-ounce tuna fillets

1] Preheat the grill and brush grate with olive oil.

2] In a small bowl, whisk together the extra virgin olive oil, lemon juice, oregano, salt, and pepper. Do not be concerned if the tastes seem strong. They are meant to be.

3] Season the tuna all over with some salt and pepper and brush with olive oil. Grill about 3 minutes per side. Transfer the tuna to platters. Spoon on the sauce and serve.

VEGETABLE SIDE DISHES

ITALIAN FARMERS ARE JUSTLY KNOWN FOR THE GLORY OF THEIR VEGETABLES. THOUGH THESE VEGETABLE DISHES MAY BE SIMPLE, THEY ARE AS LUSTY AND FULL-FLAVORED AS THE REST OF THE MEAL.

BROCCOLI WITH GARLIC

—■—

If rapini, or broccoletti di rape, is available, substitute for an even more authentic version. ✗ *Serves 6*

1 bunch (3 stalks) broccoli
3 tablespoons olive oil

3 garlic cloves, peeled and minced
Salt and freshly ground pepper

1] Trim and discard the bottom 2 inches of tough broccoli stalks. With a sharp paring knife or vegetable peeler, remove the remaining tough outer skins so the stalks are pale green. Cut the broccoli lengthwise into pieces of 3 or 4 florets each. If the stalks seem to long, cut in half along the diagonal.

2] Have ready a large mixing bowl of iced water. Bring a large saucepan of salted water to a boil and cook the broccoli until bright green and firm, about 2 minutes. With a slotted spoon transfer the broccoli to the bowl of cold water to stop cooking. Lift out and drain on paper towels.

3] Heat the oil in a large skillet over moderate heat. Cook the garlic just until the aroma is released, about 2 minutes. The garlic should not color. Add the broccoli, salt, and pepper and reduce the heat to medium-low. Cook, uncovered, about 5 minutes, stirring the pan occasionally so the garlic doesn't brown and the broccoli cooks evenly. Adjust the seasonings and serve hot.

SWISS CHARD
WITH TOMATOES AND
ROMANO CHEESE

The fresh, acidic quality of Swiss chard is accentuated beautifully in this rustic, healthy recipe from Constance Rinaldi of Queens, New York. One caveat—do not serve with a tomato-based entrée. ✀ *Serves 4*

1 head Swiss chard
3 tablespoons olive oil
2 garlic cloves, peeled and minced
1 small or ½ medium onion,
    peeled and thinly sliced
¼ teaspoon salt
1 cup (about 7) canned Italian
    peeled tomatoes, seeded and
    roughly chopped

½ teaspoon dried oregano
½ cup grated Romano cheese
¼ cup Kalamata olives, sliced off
    the pit and chopped

1] Bring a large pot of salted water to a boil. Meanwhile, prepare the Swiss chard by trimming out the tough, white inner stalks with the tip of a sharp knife. Fill your largest mixing bowl with cold tap water, submerge the leaves, and let stand for 10 minutes.

Lift the leaves out by hand and shake off excess water. You needn't pat the leaves dry since the next step is blanching. Stack a few leaves at a time, loosely roll into a cylinder, and cut along the width into 2-inch slices.

Note: This soaking technique cleans greens much more efficiently than rinsing. All the dirt settles to the bottom and you lift out sparkling greens. The key, however, is lifting the leaves out rather than using a strainer, so the dirt remains on the bottom where it belongs. Use this technique for cleaning spinach, lettuce, or any leafy green. For several heads of lettuce fill the sink rather than a bowl for soaking.

2] Blanch the chard in the boiling water just until the water returns to a rapid boil. Drain in a colander, shaking loose any excess water, and reserve.

3] Heat the olive oil in a medium saucepan over moderate heat. Cook the garlic, onion, and salt until the onion is soft and translucent, about 7 minutes. Add the tomatoes and oregano, lower the heat, and simmer, stirring occasionally, 10 minutes.

4] Add the reserved Swiss chard. Stir well, add the Romano cheese and olives, stir again, and cook briefly, just until the cheese melts. Serve warm in side dishes or small bowls, since the juices will run.

SPINACH SAUTÉ

Here is the quickest route to the essential tart, light taste of spinach. ✂ *Serves 6*

Two 12-ounce bunches spinach or escarole

2 tablespoons olive oil

3 garlic cloves, peeled and crushed

10 Kalamata olives, sliced off pit and roughly chopped

½ teaspoon salt

¼ teaspoon white pepper

1] Fill a sink with cold tap water. Trim the spinach stems and soak the leaves for about 10 minutes. Lift out the clean leaves by hand and shake loose any excess water. Pat dry with paper towels. Place in a large bowl for easy transport to stovetop.

2] Heat the oil in your largest skillet over moderate heat. Add the garlic and olives and cook, stirring frequently, until the garlic turns golden. Remove garlic cloves with a slotted spoon.

3] Add the spinach, salt, and pepper and turn the heat up to high. Sauté, tossing frequently, until evenly wilted and bright green, about 5 minutes. Serve.

ROASTED POTATOES
WITH SAGE

By being blanched and then roasted at high heat, these potatoes develop a soft flaky interior and a crisp golden crust, wonderful with braised or roasted meats. Feel free to substitute another fresh herb like rosemary or oregano, if it better complements your main course.

✕ Serves 4 to 6

6 white boiling potatoes (about 2½ pounds)
Olive oil
4 garlic cloves, peeled and crushed

1 tablespoon chopped fresh sage
½ teaspoon coarse salt
Freshly ground black pepper

1] Preheat the oven to 425 F.

2] Bring a large pot of salted water to a boil. Wash the unpeeled potatoes and cut into large chunks. Cook in boiling water for 2 minutes once the water returns to a boil. Drain in a colander, rinse with cold tap water, and then spread on a countertop to cool.

3] Coat a 9 x 12-inch roasting pan or baking dish with a thin layer of olive oil. Arrange the potatoes in one layer. Tuck the garlic cloves between the potatoes. Sprinkle on the sage, salt, and pepper. Drizzle with olive oil and bake, uncovered, until golden and crisp, about 50 minutes. Set aside to cool a few minutes before serving.

Potato Fennel Pancakes

Fennel adds an exotic hint of licorice to traditional potato pancakes. It is important to remove as much moisture as possible from the fennel or the pancakes will steam instead of fry. ✂ *Serves 4 to 6*

1 bulb fennel (about ½ pound), trimmed
2 large baking potatoes (about 1½ pounds), peeled
1 teaspoon fennel seeds, ground
1 teaspoon coarse salt
½ teaspoon white pepper
½ cup vegetable oil, or more as needed

1] Trim the stalks and root end off the fennel and coarsely grate the bulb in a food processor or by hand. Wrap in paper towels and squeeze out excess water.

2] Meanwhile coarsely grate the potatoes and combine in a medium mixing bowl with grated fennel, fennel seeds, salt, and pepper.

3] Heat the oil in a cast-iron skillet over medium-high heat. Drop about ⅓ cup of the potato mixture in the pan for each pancake and immediately flatten with a spatula. Fry about 4 minutes per side, or until golden brown and crisp. Transfer to paper towels to drain before serving. Add a tablespoon or 2 of oil to the pan between batches if the pancakes start burning.

FENNEL PARMESAN

Fennel is an extremely pungent, almost peppery vegetable popular all over Italy. This classic preparation can also be adapted for other hard vegetables like broccoli, cauliflower, or Swiss chard stalks. *Serves 4*

2 large fennel bulbs (about 2¼ pounds)
Salt
2 tablespoons unsalted butter
½ cup plus 2 tablespoons freshly grated Parmesan cheese

1] Preheat oven to 425 F. Lightly butter a 9 x 12-inch casserole or baking dish.

2] Bring a large pot of water to a boil. Trim the stalks and root ends off fennel and with a paring knife cut an X in each root end. Cook, uncovered, in boiling water for 20 minutes. With a slotted spoon, transfer to a large bowl of iced water to cool. Remove and discard the outer layer if it is bruised. Cut the fennel into ½-inch slices lengthwise.

3] Arrange fennel slices in a single layer in the buttered pan. Sprinkle lightly with salt, dot with butter, and scatter the Parmesan evenly over the top. Bake until the cheese is melted and golden, about 20 minutes. Serve warm or at room temperature.

BAKED GARLIC TOMATOES

Long, slow cooking brings out the unexpected sweetness of garlic and tomatoes. Baked tomatoes are wonderful spread on crostini or served alongside grilled veal chops. *Serves 4*

4 medium-sized ripe tomatoes, stems removed
3 garlic cloves, peeled and minced
4 teaspoons extra virgin olive oil
Coarse salt

1] Preheat oven to 325 F. Line a small baking tray with aluminum foil.

2] Cut the tomatoes in half across the width. Arrange, cut side up on baking tray. Sprinkle with minced garlic. Drizzle each half with olive oil and salt to taste. Bake until the skins shrink and the centers soften, 1½ hours. Serve warm or reserve at room temperature up to 4 hours.

MIXED GRILLED VEGETABLES WITH BALSAMIC VINEGAR

Some favorites from the Italian garden done on the grill. As a rule, grill vegetables after meat, when the flames have died down.

Fennel bulbs, blanched for 20 minutes and cut in ½-inch lengthwise slices

Small new potatoes with skins, blanched for 20 minutes

Red onion, cut in ½-inch horizontal slices

Bell peppers, cored, seeded, and cut in quarters lengthwise

Zucchini, cut in quarters lengthwise

Japanese eggplant with skin, trimmed and thinly sliced lengthwise

Olive oil
Salt and pepper
Balsamic vinegar

1] Preheat the grill. If using charcoal, cook over medium heat, after the flames have subsided some.

2] Brush the cut vegetables with oil all over and season with salt and pepper. Grill until lightly charred all over, being careful not to burn the vegetables. Arrange on a tray and drizzle lightly with balsamic vinegar. Serve warm or at room temperature.

Desserts

While restaurant tables may be laden with baroque creations, at home Italians are more apt to have a piece of fresh fruit or simple biscotti with their espresso. Most of these desserts reflect the preference for restraint and a light touch at the end of a meal.

LEMON THYME GRANITA

Granita, the ultimate light summer dessert, is an elegant granular ice that can be easily made in your home freezer. All it takes is a metal cake pan and spoon. Since it does take about 2 hours of intermittent attention, make it when you plan on being in the kitchen anyway. An alternate method for making granita when you can't possibly be in the kitchen that long is this: Freeze the mixture in the cake pan until solid, 3 to 6 hours. Before serving, remove from freezer and let sit 5 minutes, to soften. Break into large pieces with a blunt knife and transfer to a food processor fitted with the metal blade. Pulse until a granular slush is formed and then serve. ✖ *Serves 6*

2 cups water
½ cup sugar
1½ teaspoons finely grated lemon zest
2 sprigs fresh thyme

½ cup fresh lemon juice (about 3 lemons)
Additional thyme sprigs for garnish (optional)

1] Combine the water, sugar, lemon zest, and 2 thyme sprigs in a small heavy saucepan. Bring to a low boil, stirring frequently to dissolve the sugar. Set aside to cool for 10 minutes and then remove the thyme.

2] Pour into a round metal cake pan and stir in the lemon juice. Place in the freezer until ice crystals begin forming along the sides of the pan, about 45 minutes. Remove from the freezer and stir, breaking and combining the hardened bits of ice with the liquid. Return to the freezer and repeat this procedure at 15-minute intervals, until a granular slush is formed. It takes about 2 hours to reach the proper consistency. Serve in glass bowls or wine glasses with a small sprig of thyme across the top for decoration—flowering thyme from the garden would be very pretty. If you don't plan on serving right away, keep in the freezer in a plastic container with lid as long as 2 hours. Break up and stir the ice crystals before serving.

VARIATION. For espresso granita, dissolve 6 tablespoons sugar in 1 cup water. Add 1 cup of your strongest fresh-brewed espresso or French or Italian roast in place of the lemon juice. The method is the same. Espresso granita is traditionally served topped with whipped cream.

AMARETTO RICOTTA CHEESECAKE

Ricotta is so light and subtle, it is an excellent carrier of other flavors. Among the flavorings used here are pine nuts, raisins, and lemon zest. I prefer whole-milk ricotta for its fuller flavor, but feel free to substitute the low-fat variety. This cake tastes best the day it is made.

Serves 8 to 10

4 cups whole-milk ricotta
17 pairs imported Italian amaretti
   cookies
6 tablespoons (¾ stick) unsalted
   butter, melted
⅓ cup pine nuts
¼ cup Amaretto liqueur
½ cup golden raisins
½ cup sour cream

4 eggs
½ cup sugar
2 teaspoons grated lemon zest
1 teaspoon vanilla extract
3 tablespoons all-purpose flour
¼ teaspoon salt
Cinnamon and confectioner's
   sugar (garnish)

1] Here is a tip from Marcella Hazan for removing excess moisture from ricotta: Place the cheese in a medium skillet and cook over medium-high heat, stirring frequently, until the cheese separates into curds and most of the liquid evaporates, 10 to 15 minutes. Transfer to a fine strainer or a colander lined with cheesecloth and place over a large mixing bowl to drain for about ½ hour.

2] Butter the sides of a 9½-inch springform pan. Preheat the oven to 325 F.

3] Grind the amaretti cookies in a food processor with the metal blade until fine. The yield should be about 1½ cups of fine crumbs. Combine with the melted butter in a medium mixing bowl and stir with a fork. Pat the mixture into the bottom of the prepared springform pan and reserve in the refrigerator.

4] Spread the pine nuts on a baking sheet and toast in the warm oven, shaking occasionally, about 4 minutes. Set aside and turn the oven up to 350 F for baking the cake.

5] In a small saucepan, heat the Amaretto, stir in the golden raisins, and reserve.

6] Transfer the drained ricotta, discarding the liquid, to a large mixing bowl. Add the sour cream, eggs, sugar, and lemon zest. Lightly beat with a wooden spoon. With a small strainer, separate the raisins and Amaretto.

Add the Amaretto and vanilla extract to the ricotta mixture and stir with a wooden spoon or beat at low speed just to combine. The batter should not be perfectly smooth. Sprinkle the flour and salt on top and beat until well combined.

7] Add the raisins along with the pine nuts to the ricotta mixture. Stir to distribute evenly.

8] Spread the batter over the crust in the pan and smooth the top. Place on a baking sheet and bake in a 350 F oven 1 hour, or until the edges are golden brown and the center feels firm when pressed. Set aside to cool on a cake rack about 30 minutes.

9] Run a paring knife along the sides to loosen, and remove the sides of the pan. Transfer to a cake plate, leaving on the pan bottom. Garnish by sprinkling the top first with cinnamon and then with confectioner's sugar. A handy trick for sprinkling is to shake the cinnamon or sugar through a fine strainer.

QUICK AND EASY DESSERTS

These quick preparations are ideal after you've worked all day but yearn to put something more personal than packaged cookies on the table for dessert.

STRAWBERRIES IN BALSAMIC VINEGAR

✗ *Serves 4*

1 pint strawberries
2 teaspoons sugar

1 tablespoon balsamic vinegar

Stem the strawberries and cut in quarters. Arrange in a pretty glass or ceramic serving bowl. Sprinkle with sugar and vinegar and toss well to combine. Cover with plastic wrap and marinate at room temperature up to 2 hours.

ICE CREAM AND AMARETTI

For each small bowl of ice cream, crush 1 pair of amaretti (almond cookies) into rough chunks by placing the cookies in a bag and running a rolling pin lightly over the surface. Sprinkle on top of ice cream and serve. Amaretti are especially delicious with vanilla ice cream.

GRILLED PINEAPPLE
WITH RUM

✕ *Serves 6*

1 pineapple   ¼ cup rum
1 tablespoon sugar

A perfect ending to summer barbecues. Trim the pineapple ends and remove the skin. Cut across the width into ½-inch-thick circles. Core each circle and remove the eyes. Place in a cake pan or ceramic dish and sprinkle with sugar. Drizzle with rum and reserve at room temperature 1 hour. On a preheated grill, over medium flame, grill until marks appear and the fruit softens, about 3 minutes per side. Serve warm from the grill with knife and fork.

FIGS AND HONEY

Figs, with skins   Honey

Cut the figs in half lengthwise, or keep whole if small or overripe. Grill over medium-low flame until soft and warm, about 3 minutes per side. Place on plates, cut side up, and drizzle lightly with honey. Serve warm.

BAKED APPLES ON
THE GRILL

This authentic Neapolitan dessert comes from chef Antonio Orlando of Glendale, California.

Tart apples, such as Granny Smith

Wrap the apples in aluminum foil. When the fire has died but the ashes are still warm, bury apples in coals. Cook about 20 minutes. Cut out the core at the top and serve warm with spoons.

Books on Italian Cuisine and Culture

If the number of books on Italian cooking is any indication, the American love affair with Italian food shows no signs of abating. Here is a list of personal favorites for continuing your education in the Italian kitchen.

Boni, Ada. *Italian Regional Cooking*. Bonanza Books, New York, 1969.

The forerunner of today's lavishly illustrated coffee table cookbooks, this collector's item may look outdated but the content is timeless. The recipes and text provide an unchanging picture of the great variety of Italian cuisine by that nation's most respected food writer. Recipes a bit vague for the beginner.

Bugialli, Giuliano. *The Fine Art of Italian Cooking*. Times Books, New York, 1977; updated 1989.

————. *Classic Techniques of Italian Cooking*. Simon & Schuster, New York, 1982.

————. *Foods of Italy*. Stewart, Tabori & Chang, New York, 1984.

Bugialli, "the world's foremost authority on Italian cooking" according to his book's jacket copy, has a loyal following. He covers much the same ground as Hazan but with a more scholarly approach. His coffee table book, *Foods of Italy*, remains the most useful of the big, beautiful books.

David, Elizabeth. *Italian Food*. Harper & Row, New York, 1963; reissued and updated 1987.

By the renowned British food writer, this coffee table book is filled with good historical research and standard regional recipes. Buy it more for the narrative and the fun of looking at old engravings, advertising art, package labels, and postcards than for the recipes, which lack such details as ingredient lists and oven temperatures and times.

Field, Carol. *The Italian Baker*. Harper & Row, New York, 1985.

The definitive book on Italian baking in America, this impressive volume is both a resource for professional bakers and an inspiration for beginners. The author spent two years researching in Italy before painstakingly adapting each bread, breadstick, pizza, focaccia, cake, tart, and cookie recipe in her American kitchen three ways: for hand mixing, electric mixer, and food processor.

Harris, Valentina. *Recipes From an Italian Farmhouse*. Simon & Schuster, New York, 1989.

This glossy picture book captures in photography and thought the soul of Italian peasant cooking. Rustic, hard-to-find ingredients like hare, pigeon, and pig's feet, however, may mean this book rarely makes the trip into the kitchen. Exquisite photography of people, farmland, and markets for the Italophile.

Hazan, Marcella. *The Classic Italian Cook Book*. Alfred A. Knopf, New York, 1976.
———. *More Classic Italian Cooking*. Alfred A. Knopf, New York, 1978.
———. *Marcella's Italian Kitchen*. Alfred A. Knopf, New York, 1986.

Hazan is the next best thing to having an Italian mother at your side in the kitchen. Her friendly, pragmatic voice paved the way for a true understanding and appreciation of Italian food in America. The recipes are elegant, pared down, and confident without a single extra step or ingredient. And they are foolproof. Each book builds on the last, reflecting the American audience's increased sophistication and the availability of a wider range of ingredients.

La Place, Viana, and Kleiman, Evan. *Cucina Fresca*. Harper & Row, New York, 1985.
———. *Pasta Fresca*. William Morrow, New York, 1988.
———. *Cucina Rustica*. William Morrow, New York, 1990.

Elegant and easy recipes celebrating rustic southern Italian home cooking—with a California twist. Lots of marinating, grilling, and "healthy" ingredients. These eminently cookable recipes hold an accurate mirror up to current eating trends—on the West Coast anyway.

Lo Monte, Mimmetta. *Classic Sicilian Cooking*. Simon & Schuster, New York, 1990.

This very personal book offers the perspective of a Sicilian immigrant to New York, circa 1965, through diaries, family photographs, interviews and, oh yes, recipes. The recipes—thoroughly authentic, traditional renditions of southern Italian home cooking—are sometimes lengthy.

Pellegrini, Angelo. *The Unprejudiced Palate*. North Point Press, Berkeley, 1984; originally published 1948.

This charming discourse by a West Coast English professor who emigrated to this country in 1914 is filled with the wonder of the recent immigrant. At first he is awed at America's abundance and then he is amazed at our waste. In the land of TV dinners, he advises Americans to learn how to cook real food as a means to spiritual survival. Although there are no recipes, the book is filled with ideas and inspiration for simple, daily meals.

Romer, Elizabeth. *The Tuscan Year.* Atheneum, New York, 1985.

A diary of the year this British author spent in a small village between Umbria and Tuscany, looking over the shoulder of a family cook. With great attention to detail, Romer places the food in relation to the people who cook it and the places they inhabit. Recipes are interwoven with journal entries à la M.F.K. Fisher.

Root, Waverley. *The Food of Italy.* Vintage Books, New York, 1971.

Root was an American foreign correspondent with abundant appetites, both for food and description. This classic, organized according to region, is part travelogue and part history lesson. It catalogues all of the foods of Italy, with enough description for experienced cooks to re-create some dishes. A wonderful resource for planning a trip to Italy.

Simeti, Mary Taylor. *Pomp and Sustenance.* Alfred A. Knopf, New York, 1989.

Simeti, an American married to a Sicilian, weaves the story of twenty-five centuries of Sicilian cooking with recipes and personal anecdotes in a light, readable style. The recipes for the authentic foods of the island are more than mere arcana. They are well-tested, practical dishes that appeal to today's tastes. Illustrated with old engravings and black-and-white photos.

INDEX